D0642440

WEDDING
JOURNALS
& *Keepsake Gifts*

QUARRY

WEDDING JOURNALS

JOURNALS

& Keepsake Gifts

PROJECTS TO MAKE AND SHARE

Tammy Kushnir

BEVERLY MASSACHUSETTS

QUARRY BOOKS

First published in the United States of America by
Quarry Books, a member of
Quayside Publishing Group
100 Cummings Center
Suite 406-L
Beverly, Massachusetts 01915-6101
Telephone: (978) 282-9590
Fax: (978) 283-2742
www.quarrybooks.com

Library of Congress Cataloging-in-Publication Data
Kushnir, Tammy.
 Wedding journals and keepsake gifts : creative projects to make and share / Tammy Kushnir.
   p. cm.
 ISBN 1-59253-460-0
 1. Handicraft. 2. Wedding decorations. 3. Bridal books. I. Title.
 TT149.K88 2008
 745.9--dc22

                    2008007753

ISBN-13: 978-1-59253-460-9
ISBN-10: 1-59253-460-0

10 9 8 7 6 5 4 3 2 1

Design: Rachel Fitzgibbon
Cover Image: Tammy Kushnir

Printed in China

CONTENTS

INTRODUCTION

July 27, 2005

When I was given the opportunity to write a book and design the artwork, I was thrilled but nervous to the core. My father encouraged me to "think like a newlywed," by remembering the days before and after my own wedding. It wasn't easy to do while juggling young children and trying to find time to work, but it proved to be good advice.

One day, things seemed to click. I looked at my husband and my boys and the truth of marriage, and the whole wedding experience came together. I began to remember the fun I had searching for halls to hold the reception and the places I went to seek out favors for guests. I remember the catalogs I searched, trying to find that special gift for the bridal party. The projects that fill these pages are intended to help and inspire you, as you create and plan the albums and gifts that will mark and document your own special day.

Making your own albums and mementos will not only save you oodles of money, it allows you to share a piece of your artistic self with your family and friends in a gift that they will always cherish. The projects that fill these pages range from simple to a bit beyond, but they are all achievable, even if you have little art experience.

Whether you are preparing for your own wedding or looking back after the wedding to record your fond memories, my simple wish for you is to relax and be creative!

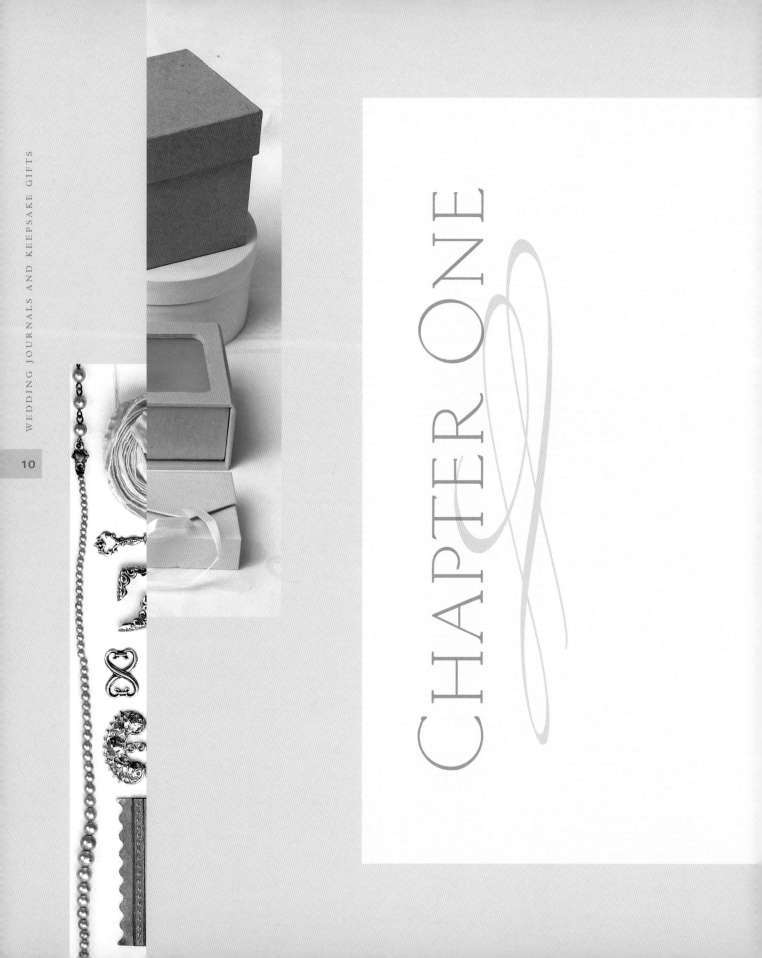

CHAPTER ONE

Getting Started

BEGINNING A NEW PROJECT often requires patience, an open mind, and many, many supplies. Although the first two requirements must come from within (and are often a challenge, especially for nervous brides-to-be), the last is often simpler to accomplish than you might think. Many of the supplies needed to make beautiful things are already in your home: brads, safety pins, even paper clips. Most of us have printers and paper and a plethora of photos waiting to be embellished. As for books to alter or boxes to decorate, a trip to a local Saturday flea market can solve that problem. Never underestimate your initial instincts about what might look great in a piece of art. Art is subjective, and beauty can be found in everything and anything. Trust yourself, and begin the adventure!

Choosing Your Style

First, a word about creative style: it is relative to each artist. Feel free to adapt these projects to suit your own color, texture, and style preferences. Are you drawn to a clean, crisp, contemporary style, or perhaps you prefer something more romantic, Victorian, or retro? Do you enjoy creating layers of texture and embellishments? The works featured here vary from fragile and delicate to edgy and bursting with color. Style your projects in any way you wish! When it comes to papers, paint colors, or embellishments, you can choose what you like. It is as simple as that.

What You'll Need

Following is a list of basic tools that you will find helpful to have on hand.

Tools

- **adhesives** You will find many different types of adhesives, and some work better than others for specific needs. Keep a selection of adhesives, such as tape runners, double-sided tape, foam dots, glue sticks, and collage glues such as Mod Podge, on hand. Glues labeled as archival, photo safe, acid free, and clear drying work well for adhering images, such as wedding photos, which you will want to preserve for future generations (**B**, **C**).

- **awl** This sharp tool can aid you in many tasks, from punching holes to placing brads (**F**).

- **brushes** If you don't already have brushes, buy a package of standard paint brushes for acrylic paints in various sizes. You might also want to purchase a few fine-detail brushes and larger fan brushes (great for feathered effects), because they will come in handy at one time or another (**H**). Stock a few inexpensive sponge brushes, for applying paint to large areas quickly (**K**).

- **cutting tools** For cutting fine details, I like Kai scissors. They not only work well for cutting rubber, they also cut curves beautifully and are great for getting into those hard-to-reach spots when you're cutting images from photographs. Deckle scissors will give your projects a decorative edge. A craft knife or box cutter can be used along with a cutting mat and ruler to cut heavier matte board or thick albums and book covers (**E**, **G**).

- **needle and thread** These are useful for sewing fabrics into your projects (**A**, **I**).

- **paints** Water-based acrylic paints are used for the projects in this book. Acrylic paints dry quickly and are nontoxic and easy to clean up with soap and water. They are also relatively inexpensive and come in many colors (**D**).

- **writing utensils** A selection of nice fine-tipped pens, colored markers, and pencils can be used for journal writing, photo captions, and your personal correspondence (**J**).

A

B

C

D

E

F

G

H

I

J

K

Supplies

The following supplies are used to make the projects in this book.

- **book board** This sturdy board is good for album covers.

- **brads** The handy accessories stylishly attach layers.

- **illustration board and bristol board**

- **images** Gather vintage and current family photos. Collage CDs filled with vintage images are inexpensive and you can use the images over and over again (see Resources on page 110).

- **items to alter, such as boxes and photo albums** Don't shy away from boxes that already have images. Much of the fun of altering is in redesigning the surface and finding new uses for what you have on hand.

- **patterned paper** Paints are wonderful, but sometimes a project needs a little boost, and patterned paper can provide that boost. Using just a little of this type of paper can take any project to the next level.

- **safety pins** These work well for attaching tags and embellishments.

- **ribbon** You can use modern ribbons from craft stores or vintage ribbon for an elegant touch.

Embellishments

There is an almost endless supply of embellishments available. Craft stores carry a huge assortment, but you can also find them in unusual places, such as flea markets, office supply stores, and even around your house. When pondering what to use, be creative and open to new ideas. Objects often present themselves when least expected.

- **buttons** Antique stores are a great source for old and unique buttons.

- **charms** Dig into your jewelry box or find charms at craft stores.

- **flea market finds** I have found some of the most interesting things at flea markets. You never know what you'll come home with!

- **old jewelry** Adding a family member's forgotten necklace or beads from a bracelet can give spark and charm to a piece.

- **rub-ons** Also called transfers, these can range in style from cute to artsy. When you find your style, you can add one or more to spice up your piece. If you are feeling adventurous, try your hand at making your own rub-ons! (See following.)

- **rub-ons transfer film** You can make your own rub-ons using Grafix Rub-Onz transfer film. The process is simple: just print an image onto the rub-on paper with an inkjet printer (you can also use a laser printer), being sure to reverse the image first, so it doesn't print backwards. Then place a piece of adhesive (included with the paper) over the image. Wait several minutes for the image to set, then cut it out and rub it onto the surface of your choice. You can also use rubber stamps to create images, or, if you are feeling creative, you can draw your own images onto the paper for a one-of-a-kind look!

- **vintage flowers** Use to add a lovely retro touch.

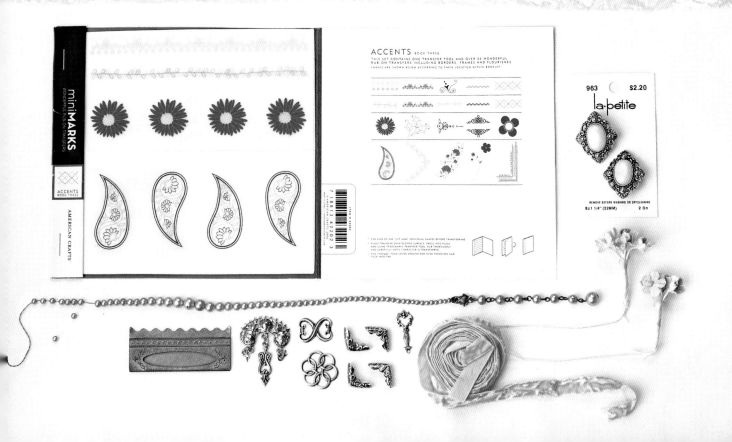

re you there?
she whispered.
m right here…
st reach out and
hold your hand.

CHAPTER TWO

For the Couple

YOU ARE GETTING MARRIED. You can feel your hands trembling from the excitement and nervousness. You often find yourself daydreaming of what marriage will be like. Every thought and image seems to hold more meaning for you now than ever before. You want to remember it all. You want to write it down and share the images with your family, friends, kids, and even grandkids! How do you begin to fulfill your creative urges? The answer is to start at the beginning, when the relationship first began.

Grow old along with me! The best is yet to be.

— Robert Browning

Tips

- If you were childhood sweethearts, add photos from your youth to look back on with fondness!

- This history book included images of children. If your history does not include children, leave some blank pages for images to come, or add images and reminders of favorite dates that you had along the way.

Our History Accordion Book

Materials

- accordion book with holder (approximate size 5" x 6 ½" [12.7 x 16.5 cm] shown)
- decorative buttons
- pewter twig
- rub-ons
- Grafix Rub-Onz transfer film
- charm
- brown and black colored pencils
- card stock (red and gray)
- patterned paper
- Victorian scrap
- hemp cord
- collage images and personal photos
- vintage beads
- library pocket
- brown marker
- newsprint paper
- utility knife
- tape
- piece of fishing line
- awl
- scissors
- glue
- glossy photo paper
- computer and printer
- Microsoft Bradley Hand ITC font in bold, or similar

All couples have history. Some might have ten years, and some might have two. No matter what the length of the relationship, each couple has a story to tell. Creating a book about the history you have experienced can be an exciting way to share your ideas for the future to come.

For the cover of the accordion holder (below):

1. Remove the paper buttons from the accordion book holder and replace them with decorative buttons, using hemp cord to secure them to the holder. (If necessary, use glue for extra security.) Use another piece of cord as a closure.

2. Add a pewter twig and a rub-on to the right-hand flap.

3. For the inside cover, adhere patterned paper to both sides of the small top and bottom flaps. Adhere cardstock to the back of the large flaps.

For the cover of the accordion book (previous page):

1. Cut a rectangular piece from the cover page of the book. Cut out an image of a wedding couple and adhere it behind the opening.

2. Add rub-ons and sketch lines around the image with a brown marker and a brown pencil. Sketch a design in each corner with a brown marker. Copy a quote and change the font to Microsoft Bradley Hand ITC in bold or a similar font.

3. Print the quote in reverse onto the rub-on film. (Note: Follow the directions included with the film.) Apply the quote beneath the image of the couple. Draw a block around the quote.

4. Glue vintage beads next to the quote.

(continued)

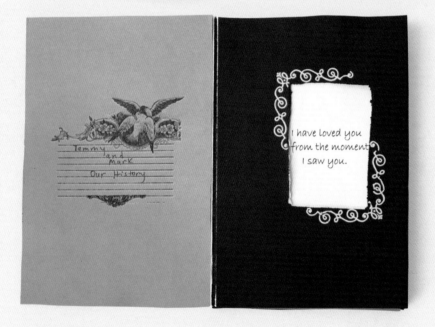

2. Cut a piece of red card stock to fit the book page. Set aside. Cut a rectangular window from the right-hand page of the book, then place the red card stock underneath the window and trace the outline onto the card stock. Cut this window from the card stock, cutting just inside the tracing lines, to create a frame for the quote.

3. Glue the card stock onto the accordion book page.

4. Print a computer-generated quote onto paper and cut it out, being sure to cut the paper large enough to fit behind the frame. Adhere it behind the window. Add rub-ons to frame the quote.

For the first spread:

Note: For this book, you will need to cut several pieces of red and gray card stock and adhere them to the accordion pages, alternating colors on each page. You will also need to cut several pieces of red card stock to adhere to the backs of the pages, over the adhered photos.

1. Cut a piece of gray card stock to fit the book and adhere it to the left-hand page of the spread. Add a rub-on and write the name of the couple and the title of the book ("Our History").

5. Cut a piece of red card stock and adhere it to the back of the book page, to cover the back of the quote. Do this for each spread, except the last page.

6. Finally, use a black pencil to draw a line down the center fold between the pages. Do this for each spread.

For the second spread:

1. For the left-hand page, follow the instructions for step 2 in the first spread, but use gray card stock and adhere a collage image behind the window.

2. Add rub-ons.

3. For the right hand page, follow the instructions for step 2 in the first spread, adhering a photo of the wedding couple behind the window.

4. Add text and rub-ons as desired.

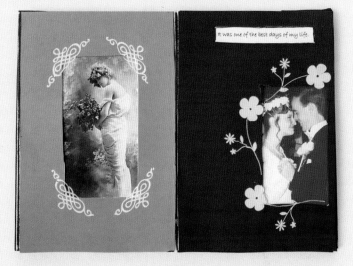

For the third spread:

1. For the left-hand page, adhere a photo of a man and baby behind the window.

2. Add rub-ons and text as desired.

3. For the right hand page, adhere a photo of a baby behind the window.

4. Add rub-ons around the images for decoration.

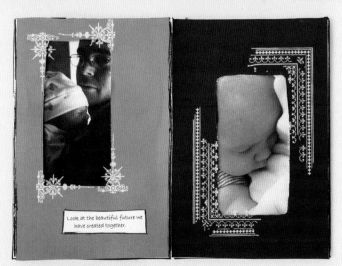

For the fourth spread:

1. Glue a library card pocket to the left-hand page. Add rub-ons to the card stock and the pocket.

2. Adhere a piece of Victorian scrap to the pocket and add the words "Along the way …" with black marker.

3. Add a charm to a piece of fishing line and tie the line around the completed book.

BLUSHING BRIDE'S DIARY

Materials

- rectangular board book (4" x 6" [10.2 x 15.2 cm] shown)
- light brown acrylic paint
- brown marker
- pencils
- white pastel pencil
- decorative rub-ons
- letter rub-ons
- sketch paper
- transparency film*
- tea bags and hot water
- sponge brush
- glue
- scissors
- deckle scissors
- template (below)

* Transparency film is a clear plastic film, often used in overhead projectors. You can find inkjet-compatible sheets online or in art and craft stores, such as A.C. Moore.

This small book is designed to hold the most intimate thoughts and feelings of the bride to be. Whether you are completely nervous or extremely joyful about the upcoming event, you can use this diary to record all of your emotions. Feelings are what help us connect to our creative selves, so write away!

For the cover:

1. Paint the cover of an unfinished board book with brown acrylic paint (see the sidebar on page 37, for more on painting backgrounds).

2. Draw onto the cover a loose sketch of a bride or photocopy and trace the template provided below. Color the dress with a white pastel pencil. Add a rub-on for the veil. Use a marker to draw lines around the bride, with swirls at the edges.

3. Add a rub-on to the spine of the book.

4. Draw a heart in each corner and color it in with a colored pencil.

5. Using rub-on letters, apply the word "Diary" beneath the drawing. Trim a piece of transparency film to fit over the drawing and lettering, to protect it. Once it is sized and positioned correctly, smear a dab of Mod Podge glue over the film with a brush and place it carefully over the drawing.

(continued)

Tips

- Feel free to sketch your own designs instead of using rub-ons; remember, this is your diary!

- Add pockets into which you can place notes or findings that remind you of your wedding before the ceremony and after.

For the inside:

1. Cut sketch paper slightly smaller than the book and adhere it to the inside front and inside back covers of the book. Add a rub-on to the bottom left hand corner of the inside front cover.

2. Cut two pieces of paper for each board book page. Cut the pages a bit larger than the actual page size, so that they fit once they have been trimmed. Use standard scissors to cut out the pages, then trim with deckle scissors for a decorative edge.

3. Glue one sheet of deckled paper to each side of the board book pages and add a rub-on for decoration at the top.

4. Tea stain each page, using a sponge brush. (See the sidebar for more on tea staining.)

Tea Stain Technique

This is a simple technique using products that can be found in most homes. First, boil some water. Once the water is boiled, pour it into a medium-sized bowl. Add tea bags to the bowl and let steep for approximately 10 to 15 minutes. (For a darker stain color, steep longer or use more tea bags. Make your mixture strong and test the color. If it's too dark, you can easily dilute it.)

Dip paper, one piece at a time into the liquid, being sure to cover the whole page, and let soak for at least five minutes (or longer, depending on how dark you want the paper to be). Alternatively, you can apply the stain to the paper with a sponge brush.

Lay the stained paper onto paper towels and allow it to dry completely before using or adding embellishments.

Keepsake Wedding Album

Materials

- white, pink, gray, green, tan, rose, and blue acrylic paints
- vintage cabinet card photo album (this one was from eBay and measured 9" x 12" [22.9 x 30.5 cm]) *
- vintage images and quotes and/or photos from the wedding (I used a quote from Enchanted Mercantile Vintage Graphics' *Victorian Ephemera* CD)
- rubber stamps with quotes
- rub-on frame to fit around quote
- ATCs *(see sidebar on page 31)*
- other decorative rub-ons
- Die Cuts with a View Vellum "Quote Stacks": Wedding & Romance
- ribbon
- patterned papers
- newsprint paper
- collage sheet image of doors
- collage sheet word: "kisses"
- label holder
- gold and pewter brads
- silver book corners
- brown marker
- adhesive foam dots
- text from a vintage book
- feathers and buttons
- glue
- scissors
- awl
- glossy photo paper
- computer and printer

* Note: if the album includes the cabinet cards, remove them from the larger page frames to leave windows in the pages.

The wedding album is the epitome of remembrances for many brides and grooms. It is often the first time that many get to see what they missed while they were greeting guests and getting pictures taken. Wedding albums are full of the greatest moments from the day, and each is truly one of a kind.

In this project, a vintage album is deconstructed and filled with photographs. When making your album, feel free to fill it solely with your own photographs. Or, if desired, add vintage images for a unique touch. Our sample pages use a mix of both. Consider devoting interior pages to your first meeting, your first date, and other landmarks of your relationship, in addition to photographs of the wedding, honeymoon, family, and friends.

For the front cover:

1. Paint a vintage cabinet card photo album with pink and white acrylic paints (see the sidebar on page 37, for more on painting backgrounds).

2. Print a vintage image of lovers and attach using adhesive foam dots.

3. Rubber stamp a romantic quote of your choosing onto the cover.

4. Add rub-ons for decoration

For the inside front and back covers (not shown):

1. Adhere patterned paper to front and back inside covers.

2. Computer-generate a quote of your choice (I used a quote from Enchanted Mercantile Vintage Graphics' *Victorian Ephemera* CD; you can also cut a quote from a collage sheet). Adjust it to fit as an inset in the rub-on frame. Test the size on a scrap sheet. Print the final quote onto photo paper and adhere it to the inside front cover.

3. Add the rub-on frame around the quote.

4. Add three flower rub-ons to the bottom of the inside front cover.

(continued)

For the "words of love" left page:

Note: To give them added thickness, pages throughout the album were doubled up. To do this, use an awl to poke holes in the top and bottom right corners of the right-hand pages—two pages at a time. Insert brads through the holes to hold the pages together. Whether you do this before or after the page is completed depends on the page treatment.

For the frame:

1. Paint the page frame using two colors, gray for the frame and pink for the borders. Add decorative rub-ons to the corners. Adhere patterned paper to the back of the frame window.

2. Add pencil lines to the frame to create texture.

For the card:

1. Insert patterned paper into the cabinet card window. Apply rub-ons to the frame of the card.

2. Print an image of a wedding couple and glue it to the patterned paper. Print and cut out a picture of a column and adhere it over the couple with adhesive foam dots.

3. Computer-generate the phrase "Words of Love" (or clip text from a vintage book), cut it out, and glue it to the card. Attach a label holder over the phrase with pewter brads.

4. With an awl, poke two holes into the card and draw a ribbon through them.

5. Adhere the finished card to the patterned paper in the frame window.

For "A Meeting," right page:

1. In the sample album, the page was sufficiently aged, so it did not need painting. If you wish, you can paint the background or age your album page with tea (see sidebar on page 24 for more on tea staining).

2. Add a rub-on to each corner.

3. Adhere patterned paper to the window in the frame.

4. Print an image or photograph of a couple and adhere it to the patterned paper using adhesive foam dots.

5. Print or cut out a phrase of your choosing. Ours is "A Meeting," from a vintage book.

6. Adhere phrase to the page. Finish the page with rub-ons.

For "Modern Love," right page:

1. Add rub-ons to the bottom corners of the page.

2. Adhere patterned paper or background images into each window.

3. For the top left window, attach a bird to the corner of the frame. Cut the word "Kisses" from a collage sheet and adhere it to the background.

4. For the top right window, adhere a small, cut-out heart above an image of a wedding couple.

5. To the background image in the bottom left window, add the phrase "An adventure" (from a vintage book) and use adhesive foam dots to adhere an image of a bride.

6. For the last window, add a rose to the background with adhesive foam dots. Add the word "love" from a vintage book underneath the window.

7. Add a button and ribbon to the center of the page.

For "Vintage Love," left page:

1. Paint the edges of the page.

2. Overstamp the page with a quote to create a background pattern on the page.

3. Add rub-ons to the left-hand corners and the middle of the right side.

4. Print or copy a vintage image of a woman and adhere it in the frame window. Stamp quote beneath the image.

5. Add silver book corners.

For "Modern Love 2," left page:

1. Paint the page.

2. Cut two Artist Trading Cards (see the sidebar on ATCs, page 31) to fit the album frames. (Note: you might need to adjust the size of the ATCs to fit the frames).

3. Print vintage images to create backgrounds and glue them to the ATCs. Cut out and adhere the main images to the cards. (We used a bird and fairy.) Draw a birdcage around the bird with a marker.

4. Add rub-ons to ATCs and insert them into two of the frames.

5. Insert two modern wedding images into the remaining frames.

6. Outline the frames with a marker and add a button and feather to the center of the page.

7. Add silver book corners.

For "Getting Ready," left page:

1. Paint only the border of the page, carefully drawing pencil lines along the sides.

2. Add rub-ons to the corners and around the frame.

3. Add patterned paper to the window to create a backdrop.

4. Adhere a quote to the background paper along with a rub-on to frame it.

5. Print and attach a vintage bride image with adhesive foam dots.

6. Add silver book corners.

For "The Wedding Party," right page:

1. Paint only the border of the page and add pencil lines around the edge.

2. Adhere a vintage button to the center of the page and add rub-ons to surround it.

3. Insert background paper into the windows. Print vintage images of a bridal party: flower girl, bridesmaid, maid of honor, and ring bearer. Adhere the images to background paper in the windows.

4. Using a word processing program, print the bridal party titles (for example, "flower girl," "bridesmaid") onto newsprint paper. (The sample uses Times New Roman font in bold and italic.) Adhere to window backgrounds.

For "Hidden Doors," left page:

1. Paint the center of the page, leaving the border plain. Draw pencil lines outlining the border.

2. Glue a feather to the center of the page.

3. Cut patterned paper to size and adhere in each window.

4. Clip sayings from the View Vellum Quote Stack and adhere to background paper in two of the windows.

5. Adhere photographs of a wedding couple to the paper in the other two windows.

6. Cut two door images from a collage sheet. Cut the doors apart at the center, so that they fold open. Glue them over the wedding couple images.

For "A New Beginning," right page:

1. Paint the center of the page, leaving the border plain. Outline the border with pencil.

2. Add rub-ons to each corner of the page.

3. Adhere a print of a bird and nest (I used Cavallini) in the window.

4. Write "A New Beginning" onto the print.

To finish the book:

1. Create additional pages as desired, devoted to the wedding party, your parents, your extended family, and your friends.

Artist Trading Cards

Along with the rising interest in all things crafts, the invention of Artist Trading Cards (commonly known as ATCs) has excited novice and experienced artists alike. These miniature works of art (no more than 2 ½" x 3 ½" [6.4 x 8.9 cm], the size of a playing card) have become a fascination for some and an obsession for many.

Their small format offers a small, nonintimidating canvas, a place to experiment with a small design in a short period of time, with little or no prep. They are great for those who have much to do (brides, for example!) but who want to create something meaningful that expresses a memory or moment they want to remember and share with family and friends. ATCs can be made using paint, collage images, fabric scraps, or even three-dimensional embellishments.

Honeymoon Journal

Materials

- blank scrapbook (8" x 6" [20.3 x 15.2 cm] shown)
- white and rust acrylic paints
- matte gel medium
- patterned paper
- rub-ons
- photos
- collage images
- Die Cuts with a View Vellum "Quote Stacks": Wedding & Romance
- black marker
- library pocket
- ribbon
- findings
- vintage millinery flowers (poppy, orange nosegay)
- inkjet compatible transparency film
- scissors
- glue
- computer and printer
- glossy photo paper

Now that the wedding celebration is over, the couple can relax and finally enjoy each other's company. The honeymoon is a perfect time for this. It is a chance to get away from the hustle and bustle of the past several months and is the first opportunity to make memories as newlyweds. Journaling during the honeymoon can help you both remember exactly what you were thinking and feeling at the time.

For the cover:

1. Cut a piece of patterned paper to fit the cover of the blank scrapbook. Leave the spine of the scrapbook blank.

2. Add a rub-on frame and insert the couple's name and date of wedding or honeymoon.

3. Adhere an image of the couple to the corner using adhesive foam dots.

4. Tie a ribbon around the completed book.

For the first spread:

1. Paint the left-hand side with rust acrylic paint (see the sidebar on page 37, for more on painting backgrounds).

2. Paint the right-hand page white. Add a rub-on and a vintage fabric flower to one corner.

3. Copy a photo of the couple and glue it to the page. Add a rub-on.

4. Highlight the corners of the photo with a black marker.

(continued)

HONEYMOON JOURNAL (CONTINUED)

For the second spread:

1. Swipe both pages of the spread with white acrylic paint to add texture.

2. Add a vellum wedding quote to the left-hand page and outline it in black marker.

3. Add a rub-on heart beneath the quote.

4. For the right-hand side, use an inkjet printer to print a map image onto a sheet of transparency film, being sure to reverse the image first, and cut out the image. Apply a thin, even layer of gel medium (such as Golden or Liquitex) to the page, then place the transparency, printed side down, onto the medium. Burnish the image with your finger or a bone folder until it has transferred to the page. (Lift the corner of the image, to see if it is transferring; if not, continue to burnish until the transfer is complete.) Once the image has transferred successfully lift off the transparency film.

5. Adhere an image of the couple to the map once it has dried.

Tips

- You can create some interesting results and discover new techniques by experimenting with different materials in your creations. For example, I used the plastic cover from a set of Martha Stewart rub-ons for the map transfer in this project and found that it worked beautifully. I printed a mirror image of the map onto the plastic, and while it was still wet, placed the image onto the page, burnishing it carefully, so it did not smear. Once the image was successfully transferred, I lifted off the plastic.

- I tested both sides of the plastic and found that one side transfers the colors better than the other. I also discovered that the image transferred completely off the plastic and onto the paper, allowing the plastic to be used again.

- If you want to try this method, use care. Although it can be fun to experiment, you should be careful with materials that will be run through the printer. The plastic I used is not designed for inkjet or laser printers and must be watched carefully, because the printer can jam.

For the third spread:

1. Swipe both pages with white acrylic paint to add texture.

2. Print an image of the couple and adhere it to the bottom left corner of the left-hand page. Glue a vellum wedding quote over the image, being sure to apply the glue sparingly.

3. Add border rub-ons around the quote.

4. Glue a small plastic pocket to the page and add a "Paris" rub-on.

5. Print a photo of the Eiffel Tower and adhere it to the right-hand page. Outline the corners of the image with a black marker.

6. Add a rub-on to the corner of the photo and one to the corner of the page.

For the fourth spread:

1. Swipe both pages with white acrylic paint to add texture.

2. Add a rub-on to the corner of the left-hand page.

3. Print an image of the groom and adhere it to the page with adhesive foam dots.

4. Place a heart rub-on next to the groom, so he appears to be leaning on the heart.

5. Print an image onto transparency film. Cut it out and glue it to the right-hand page. Add white paint around the edges of the image.

6. Add a rub-on quote to the top of the page.

For the fifth spread:

1. Paint both pages with white acrylic paint.

2. Add border rub-ons to the top and bottom of the left-hand page.

3. Add a vellum wedding quote to the center of the page and outline the corners of the quote with black marker.

4. Adhere a transparency image to the bottom of the right-hand page and outline the edges with white paint.

5. Add a rub-on design to the top of the page and a rub-on of the word "Darling."

6. Adhere an image of the bride to the transparency.

For the sixth spread:

1. Paint both pages with white acrylic paint.

2. Adhere a transparency image to the left-hand page and paint the edges in white.

3. Add a rub-on design to the bottom right corner of the right-hand page. Adhere an image of the couple over the rub-on.

4. Add a design rub-on to the top of the page and a flower rub-on to the bottom left corner. Draw a vine with flowers from the flower up to the scroll design at the top of the page. Repeat for the other side of the page. Color the flowers with blue and yellow pencils.

For the final spread:

1. Swipe both pages with white acrylic paint to add texture. Draw scroll designs around the edges of the left-hand page.

2. Glue a library pocket to the center of the page. Add hand drawn designs to the corners of the library pocket, along with the word "Travels." Add a dash of white paint to the library pocket.

3. Insert a postcard or other memorabilia from the honeymoon into the pocket. (We used a collage image for show.)

Tips

- Include lots of pockets and envelopes on each page into which the newlyweds can place goodies from the trip.

- Avoid overloading the pages with too many images. Leave some pages blank or sparsely covered, to allow room for journaling.

Painting Backgrounds

Patterned paper can make beautiful backgrounds for your projects. You can create your own unique backgrounds by painting them yourself with acrylic paints. Because acrylics are water-based, cleanup is easy, typically requiring only soap and water. The paints have little to no odor, and drying time is relatively quick.

Try mixing two or more colors together to create a new color. Adding white to any other color will lighten it up, softening the hue, so that it doesn't appear too harsh against the project at hand. A layer of white on any book page provides a nice, light-colored background to work on. To create a thicker application, brush the paint onto the page using a sponge brush.

Textured background effects can be created by using various brush types—fan brushes, for example—as well as various brush sizes, from the smallest to the largest you can find. With practice and time, you will learn each brush's style and how to incorporate it in your art.

Mini Brag Book

Materials

- 3" x 3" mini album (2½" x 2½" [6.4 x 6.4 cm] shown)
- pressed flowers
- collage images and personal photos
- rub-ons
- patterned paper in two coordinating designs
- colored pencil
- newsprint paper
- scissors
- glue
- glossy photo paper
- computer and printer
- Microsoft Edwardian Script ITC font in bold

After the wedding, the first thing everyone will ask is: "Do you have pictures?" Sometimes we can say yes, but often we sadly shake our heads no. The wait for photos from the professional photographer can be lengthy—and frustrating. A mini brag book, filled with copies of your friends' and relatives' photos of the wedding and reception, is small enough to carry with you and is a great way to share the fun you had, while you're waiting for the professional photos to come in.

For the cover:

1. Print or copy a photograph of a wedding couple and adhere it into the square window.

2. Adhere a transparency image over the couple's image.

3. Add a rub-on to the upper corner.

For the inside cover and the first spread:

Note: The patterned paper used was double-sided. For each page, alternate between each side. Use Microsoft Edwardian Script ITC font in bold for the phrases.

1. Glue a pressed flower to both the front and the back inside covers.

2. Glue the first patterned paper onto the right-hand page. Print the phrase "I will love you …" and adhere it to the page on an angle.

3. Draw one large heart and one smaller heart using a colored pencil.

4. Add a photo of the couple.

(continued)

For the second spread:

1. Adhere the double-sided patterned paper, alternating it for each page. Add a photo of the wedding couple to each side.

2. On the left-hand page, adhere a collage image in the upper corner. Print the phrase "and honor you …" and adhere it to the page.

3. Print out the phrase "in good times and in bad …" and adhere it to the right-hand page.

For the third spread:

1. Adhere the double-sided patterned paper, alternating it for each page. On the left-hand page, add a rub-on in the upper left hand corner and adhere a photo to the bottom. Using a colored pencil, add a hand-drawn heart.

2. Print the phrase "in sickness …" and adhere it to the left-hand page.

3. Add a rub-on to the top of the right-hand page and adhere the phrase "and in health …" beneath the rub-on.

4. Complete the page with another image of the couple.

For the final spread:

1. Adhere patterned paper to the left-hand page. Print the phrase "all the days of my life" and adhere it to the top of the page.

2. Add a rub-on to the center of the page.

3. Adhere an image of the wedding couple to the bottom of the page, slightly overlapping the rub-on.

ALTERED DREAM JOURNAL

Materials

- board book with cut-out windows (6½" x 6½" [16.5 x 16.5 cm] shown)
- blue, white, rust, purple, and green acrylic paints
- leaf garland
- book corners
- vintage images
- rustic primitive heart
- pewter corner sticker
- white and blue markers
- brads
- label holder
- dollhouse Gothic windowframe
- leaf charm
- crushed velvet ribbon
- rub-ons
- patterned paper
- cardstock
- collage and transparency sheet images
- library pocket
- red, orange, and yellow pastel pencils
- drawing pencils
- vintage clips
- quote (from European Papers collage sheet: Romance Quotes #1)
- newsprint paper
- book board
- transparency film
- utility knife
- sponge brush
- Kai scissors
- glue
- awl
- glossy photo paper
- computer and printer
- 1942 type font from Enchanted Mercantile-Vintage Graphics CD: *Vintage Ephemera, Volume One*

This dream journal was created using colors, patterns, and images intended to evoke emotions brought on by dreams. While the images adorn the pages, there are sufficient areas left for the couple to write about their dreams, in any way they choose.

For the cover:

1. Use a sponge brush to paint the front and back covers blue and green, respectively (see the sidebar on page 37, for more on painting backgrounds). Sketch a swirl design (or similar) around the rectangular opening and in the corner of the front cover.

2. Cut out vintage flower images and glue them to the swirly design.

3. Attach brads to the corners.

4. Cut book board to fit the rectangular window.

5. Adhere a vintage couple image to the board. Paint around the edges.

6. Add a decorative corner sticker to the piece and write "Dare to be Passionate" in black marker. Add a rub-on of the word "Dare."

7. Cut a piece of transparency film to fit and adhere it over the piece. Insert the piece into the window.

8. Glue a primitive heart to the spine. Add a letter (in this case, S) to the heart and trace around the letter with a white drawing pencil to make it stand out.

9. Tie a leaf garland around the completed book for closure.

For the first spread :

1. Use a sponge brush to paint both sides of the spread with white acrylic paint. With an awl, poke holes into the top and bottom right corners of this and the following pages. Insert brads into the holes, to hold the pages together. Do this for all the spreads, with the exception of the third spread.

(continued)

2. Add a rub-on quote in the window.

3. Adhere an image of a woman with wings to the left-hand page and use brads to attach a strip of crushed velvet. (Note: This page can be used to hold letters or notes. Our sample letter is from a collage CD.)

4. Use a black marker to draw a pattern at the top of the left-hand page and the bottom of the right-hand page.

For the second spread:

1. Adhere patterned paper to both pages of the spread.

2. Add book corners to the left-hand page and a rub-on in the middle.

3. Glue a leaf charm to the center of the rub-on.

4. For the right-hand page, use Kai scissors or a utility knife to cut out the window. With an awl, poke holes into the top and bottom right corners of this and the following page. Insert brads into the holes, to hold the pages together.

5. Using the dollhouse window frame as a template, create a stained glass design with pastel pencils on the window background .

6. Adhere the photo of the wedding couple into the window. Glue the dollhouse window frame over them, being sure to glue it securely.

5. Add book corners to the page.

6. Using the 1942 type font, computer-generate the phrase "Dream as one" and print it out on newsprint paper. Cut out the phrase and secure it under a label holder. Attach the label holder to the page with brads.

For the third spread:

1. Using a sponge brush, paint both pages in the spread with white acrylic paint.

2. Add a rub-on across the top of both pages.

3. Make an ATC for the left-hand page and attach it with clips.

4. Add the book corners.

For the fourth spread:

1. Adhere patterned paper to both pages of the spread. With a utility knife, cut out the square windows in the right-hand page. Using an awl, poke holes into the top and bottom corners of the next two right-hand pages. Insert brads into the holes.

2. Cut out two collage sheet images and glue one into each square. Adhere a rustic house embellishment over the top left collage image . Apply a rub-on of the word "family" to the house. Add a charm of a woman to the other square.

3. Cut a quote from European Papers collage quote sheet and adhere it to the left side of the page.

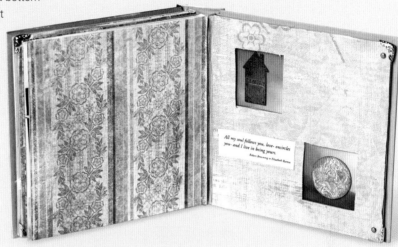

For the fifth spread:

1. Use a sponge brush to paint the left-hand page of the spread with rust acrylic paint and the right-hand page with purple acrylic paint.

2. Add a library pocket to the left-hand page to hold notes, dried flowers, and other treasures.

Making the ATC:

1. Cut cardstock to ATC size (see sidebar on page 31 for more information). Cut an image to fit the ATC and adhere it with glue.

2. Create 1942 type font and adhere it to the ATC.

3. Apply a flower rub-on over the image.

journal

Tip

This is a basic handmade book. Try researching and experimenting with other binding techniques. There are many available!

HANDBOUND DREAM JOURNAL

Materials

- book board (6" x 8" [15.2 x 20.3 cm] shown)
- book cloth
- cardstock
- ribbon
- rub-on
- patterned paper
- white computer paper
- newsprint paper
- label holder
- awl
- Mod Podge glue
- scissors
- Microsoft Times New Roman font in bold

Dreams are what make us who we are and who we want to be. Without them, we can get stuck in a world that makes demands on us every day. This is a book meant to free the personal dreams of the bride or the bride and groom as a couple. Make some quiet time and with a sweet-smelling candle and gentle music to inspire you, dream away!

For the covers:

1. Cut book board to approximately 6½" x 6½" (approximately 16.5 x 16.5 cm). Cut this piece in half to create two cover boards.

2. For the front cover, cut a piece of sturdy paper to the size of the book board, plus 1" (2.5 cm) all around. Adhere the paper to the book board with Mod Podge, being sure to center the board on the page.

3. Cut off the corners of the paper, leaving about ¼" (about 6 mm) between the book board and the edge of the paper.

4. Fold in the side flaps and glue them securely to the book board. Then fold over the top and bottom flaps and glue them down.

5. Cut a piece of patterned paper slightly smaller than the cover and glue it to the inside of the front cover, leaving a border of the cover paper around the edges.

6. Repeat steps 2 to 5 for the back cover.

7. Add a rub-on to the bottom right corner of the front cover

For the spine and pages:

1. To create the spine, first sandwich your pages (see step 2) between the covers to determine the size of the spine. Cut a piece of book cloth to fit and glue it to the covers, overlapping the cover paper by about 1½" (3.8 cm) on each cover.

2. For the pages, use paper from a previously purchased album or stack several sheets and fold them in the center, using a bone folder if necessary. Unfold the pages, so you have a stack with the fold down the middle, align them with the spine, then use the awl to make holes through all the pages and the spine at once, so the holes align. (Note: If the stack of pages is too thick, poke the holes in the top page and use it as a template.)

3. From the inside, pull the ribbon through the top two holes and braid it through the holes and down the spine. Leave excess ribbon to fall at the end, for use as a bookmark.

4. Print the word "Journal" in Times New Roman font onto newsprint paper, cut it out, and insert it into a label holder. Attach the label holder to the back cover.

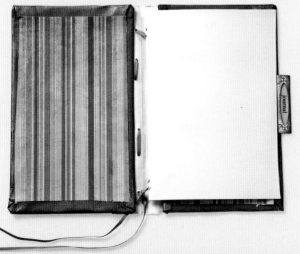
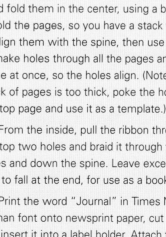

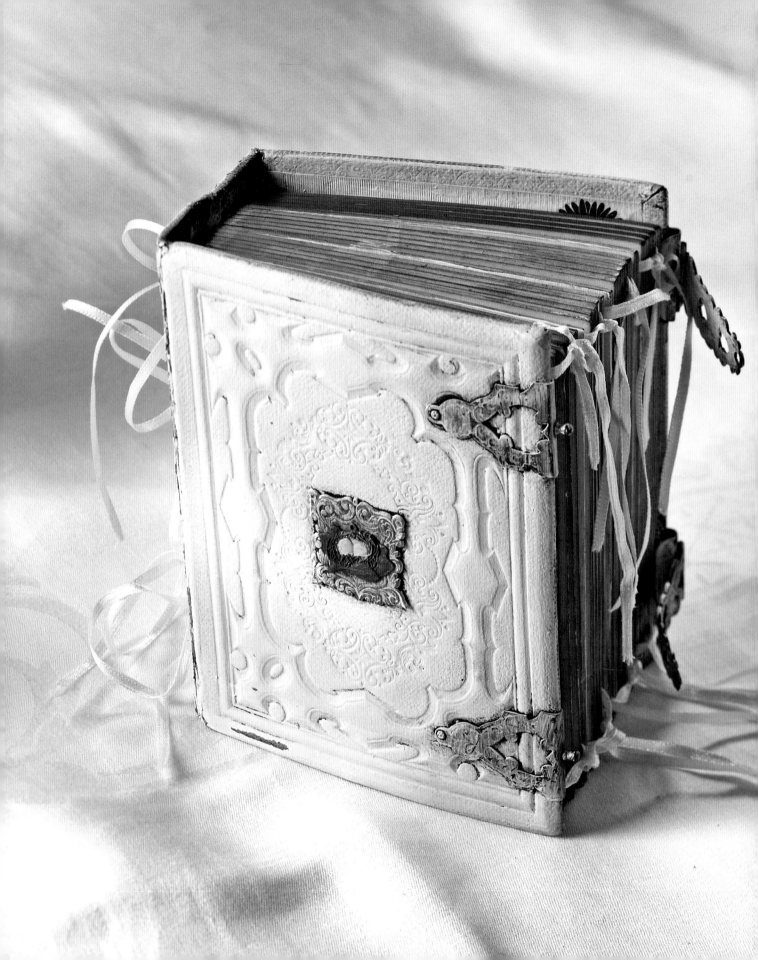

THE NEST JOURNAL

Materials

- small vintage cabinet card photo album (6" x 6" [15.2 x 15.2 cm] shown)
- white, brown, and blue acrylic paints
- small bird's nest charm
- ribbon
- vintage images
- rub-ons
- Die Cuts with a View Vellum "Quote Stacks": Wedding & Romance
- patterned paper
- glue
- sponge brush
- fine-tipped brush
- scissors
- awl
- glossy photo paper
- computer and printer

This small journal is filled with vintage images of brides and grooms, lovers, and couples. It is a place in which to hide personal treasures and words of love from husband and wife, to be treasured well into old age, when they realize they could never have made this journey without each other.

For the album cover:

1. Using a sponge brush, paint the front, inside, and back covers of the vintage album in white acrylic paint (see the sidebar on page 37, for more on painting backgrounds).

2. Use a fine-tipped brush to paint the nest of a bird's nest charm with brown paint and the eggs with blue. Adhere the charm to the center of the cover.

3. Use the awl to punch three sets of two holes through the album pages and the spine. (If this is difficult, you might want to remove the cover and punch holes through the spine and pages separately, being careful to align the holes.)

4. Cut three pieces of ribbon. Pull each piece through each pair of holes and tie it securely into a bow.

   Note: For each spread gather three album pages and with an awl, poke holes in the top and bottom right-hand corners of the bottom two pages. Tie ribbon through the holes—but not too tightly—to hold the pages together. This allows the pages to be opened, so that letters and mementoes of the couple's journey together can be placed inside. Each spread will consist of a "stack" of three pages: one single page on top and two bundled pages following.

(continued)

Tip

Instead of using vintage images, use photos from the wedding or of your ancestors. It adds character and charm!

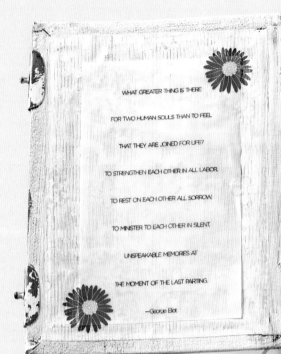

For the first spread, "The Bride":

1. For the left-hand page, cut a quote about weddings from the vellum quote book and adhere it to the center of the page. Add two rub-ons to the page.

2. For the right-hand page, print out or copy two images of the same column (reverse one image). Cut them out and adhere one over the window of the top page. Flip the page over and slide the second column reverse image into the window frame, over the first column, so that the page is sandwiched between them. This hides the back of the printed image.

3. Print out or photocopy an image of a woman and insert it into the window of the second page of the stack. (Attaching the image to the second page gives depth to the completed design.) Add rub-ons to the top and bottom corners of the page.

4. Cut a piece of decorative paper to fit and slide it into the window of the bottom page of the three-page stack.

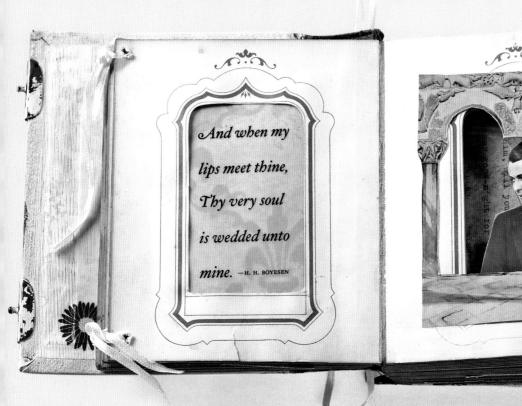

And when my lips meet thine, Thy very soul is wedded unto mine. —H. H. BOYESEN

For the second spread, "The Groom":

1. Insert a piece of patterned paper into the window of the left-hand page. Insert a vellum quote into the window, sliding it carefully over the patterned paper.

2. For the right-hand page, print out or photocopy two images of the same column and repeat the instructions for step 2 of the previous spread.

3. Slide an image of a groom into the window of the second page of the three-page stack. Add rub-ons to the page.

4. Insert patterned paper into the window of the bottom page

For the third spread, "The Lovers":

1. Insert a piece of patterned paper into the window of the left-hand page. Insert a vellum quote into the window, sliding it carefully over the patterned paper.

2. Cut out an image of trees and adhere it to the right-hand top page, carefully cutting out the window in the center. Leave the back side of the page blank.

3. Insert an image of lovers into the window of the second page of the three-page stack. Add rub-ons to the page.

4. Insert patterned paper into the window of the bottom page.

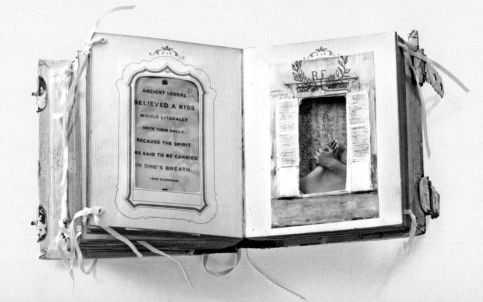

For the fourth spread, "Growing Old":

1. Insert a piece of patterned paper into the window of the left-hand page. Insert a vellum quote into the window, sliding it carefully over the patterned paper.

2. For the right-hand top page, cut two images of a window with shutters from a collage CD and carefully cut out the centers. Adhere one window piece over the opening in the page. Flip the page and slide the second window image into the frame of the top page. (Remember to reverse the image.)

3. Insert a photo of holding hands into the window of the second page of the three-page stack. Add rub-ons to the page.

4. Insert patterned paper into the window of the bottom page.

For the final spread:

1. Insert a piece of patterned paper into the window of the left-hand page.

2. Cut a quote from the vellum quote book and adhere it to the inside back cover. Add rub-ons to the opposite corners.

CHAPTER THREE

For the Big Day

IT'S NEVER TOO SOON TO START THINKING ABOUT THE DETAILS. Your dreams are quickly becoming reality. Where should you have the reception? What flowers will look best? How much should you spend on a wedding dress? To keep wedding details from becoming overwhelming, it helps to be organized. The ideas presented in this chapter will inspire you to create your own wedding planners. You'll also find ideas for creating party books to remember the special guests who shared these moments with you.

Tips

- Choose a book that is right for the bride's needs. It should be large enough to hold a lot of information and durable enough to survive the many trips it will take.

- Dress up the planner with dates, words, and other materials from your local scrapbook or craft store.

BRIDAL PLANNER

Materials

- accordion portfolio (9¾" wide x 1" deep x 12.5" high [24.8 x 2.5 x 31.8 cm] shown)
- window pocket
- ornate letter rub-on
- design rub-on
- glue

For the interior:

- cardstock
- grey patterned paper
- collage images
- brads and label holder
- rub-ons
- small gold photo turns
- clip
- black marker

All brides need to plan and this planner makes it easy to keep track of things. Simple and modern, it also has a touch of business sense, with plenty of space to hold receipts, photos of dresses, and more.

For the planner:

1. Glue a window pocket to the top of the portfolio case.

2. Apply an ornate letter rub-on to the front of the window pocket. (You can choose the letter of your last name—or your new one, for that matter.)

3. In the corner, add a design rub-on.

4. Fill the interior page as desired. For this example, I used some collage images of possible places to go for a honeymoon. Seeing visual samples can help make your goal seem that much more attainable. Also included is a place to hold business cards or receipts, as well as paper to list vacation costs.

POCKET PLANNER

Materials

- 3 ½" x 4 ½" ribbon closure box (3" x 3" [7.6 x 7.6 cm] shown) in the color of your choice
- blue, cream, and gray acrylic paints
- rub-ons
- Grafix Rub-Onz transfer film
- collage image
- clips
- bristol board
- art paper
- hemp cord
- patterned paper
- tag
- black marker
- fan brush
- scissors
- awl
- glue

Having a large planner to hold all your bridal notes is great but for on the go consider using a pocket planner. The pocket planner provides a small but decorative place to store your ideas and all the information you need for planning the wedding. It will help to make this major life event seem less overwhelming.

For the box:

1. Add decorative rub-ons to the edges of the ribbon box and a ring rub-on in the center of the top flap.

2. Cut bristol board to fit and glue the pieces to the inside flaps of the box. Paint the bristol board with blue, cream, and gray acrylic paint, alternating colors with the fan brush (see the sidebar on page 37, for more on painting backgrounds).

3. Draw and create your own rub-ons using Grafix Rub-Onz transfer film (follow directions supplied with the transfer film) and apply them to the painted board.

4. Cut a piece of patterned paper and glue to the bottom of the box.

5. Cut another piece of bristol board to fit the opening of the box. Cut a collage image to size and glue it to one side of the board. Cut a piece of the patterned paper to size and glue it to the back of the bristol board.

6. Use an awl to poke two holes in the box, one at each side. Insert clips into the holes to hold the collage image. The collage piece acts as the door to your planner.

(continued)

For the book:

1. Cut a 7" X 3" (17.8 x 7.6 cm) piece of art paper and accordion fold it to fit into the box.

2. Write the word "Planner" on the front of the folded paper with a black marker. Punch two holes into the paper, pull the hemp cord through and tie it.

3. Apply a rub-on of your own design to a tag and attach it to the hemp cord.

Tip

For a new spin, try your hand at making your own rub-ons instead of buying them. Although it requires patience, creating your own rub-ons can be a lot of fun. You can use your computer to print an image onto the transfer film, or you can create your own designs. Start with simple images, such as hearts and swirls, or use your own handwriting or printing. Rub-ons add a glossy effect to the images and will make your own writing stand out against photos. Remember to reverse your design, so that it comes out correctly when applied.

ad infinitum *(adv.)* to infinity.

WEDDING GUEST BOOK

Materials

- book for altering (5" x 7 ½" [12.7 x 19.1 cm] shown)
- four pieces of book board, cut to size (approximately 5" x 7 ½" [12.7 x 19.1 cm])
- white, pink, blue, and green acrylic paints
- pencil
- purple, red, green, and brown colored pencils
- brown marker
- images of eggs and butterflies
- image of wedding hands
- rub-ons
- flower embellishments
- vintage fabric (white field daisies)
- vintage dictionary pages
- patterned paper
- ribbon
- buttons
- safety pins
- sponge brush
- tea lights and brush for wax
- gold brads
- glue
- scissors
- awl
- glossy photo paper
- computer and printer

The wedding guest book is a treasure. It contains not only a record of the wedding guests but also their memories of the bride and groom as family members and friends. When creating this guest book, I looked within to find simple yet reflective images and drawings that incorporate the spirit of marriage, as well as memories of the wedding.

Creating the Covers:

1. Use a sponge brush to paint the outside front and back covers with white acrylic paint (see the sidebar on page 37, for more on painting backgrounds). For a grittier page, dab some of the excess paint off the sponge brush before applying and apply the paint roughly.

2. Add vintage dictionary pages or other book pages to the cover while the paint is still wet, then paint another layer over the pages.

3. Adhere the photo of the wedding hands to the cover. Dab paint around the edges of the photo to help it merge with the cover. Cut out and adhere the word "Infinite." Glue the flower onto the cover.

4. Paint the front and back covers with melted wax, using a flat brush. (See Tip.) Add a bit of wax to the flower, as well.

5. For the enclosure, cut two strips of ribbon, approximately 8" (20.3 cm) each. Wrap them around the cover of the completed book, leaving enough ribbon for the closure. Attach the decorative buttons to the ribbons with safety pins.

(continued)

WEDDING GUEST BOOK (CONTINUED)

For the first and fifth spreads, "Flowers":

1. Using a sponge brush, paint the inside cover and right-hand page with pink and white acrylic paints.

2. While the paint is still wet, add pieces of torn paper from the vintage dictionary to both pages of the spread. When dry, paint over the pages with a thin, uneven layer of paint, so you can see fragments of the paper beneath.

3. Adhere three flower embellishments to the borders of the left-hand page, along with some white rub-ons.

4. With brown marker (you can use a pencil first), draw vines and leaves over the rub-ons, allowing some to be seen through, then color in the leaves with colored pencils.

5. Paint the right-hand page and a piece of book board with white acrylic paint. Poke holes in the top and bottom right-hand corners of the board. Poke holes to match in the following two pages and attach the board and pages together with gold brads. (The board opens on left-hand side, to hold notes or cards for the couple from the guests.)

6. Add a piece of writing (perhaps some words with meaning) to the book board and paint it again lightly.

7. Use a pencil to draw a flower pattern in the lower right corner. Trace over the pattern with marker and color it in with pencils.

For the second spread, "The Cake":

1. Using a sponge brush, paint the left-hand page in blue acrylic paint.

2. Cut two hearts from patterned paper and adhere them to the left-hand corners.

3. Add a rub-on in the center and along the top and bottom, connecting the hearts.

4. Paint the right-hand page and a piece of book board with white acrylic paint. Poke holes in the top and bottom right-hand corners of the board. Poke holes to match in the following two pages and attach the board and pages together with gold brads.

5. On the bottom right side of the book board, draw a simple sketch of a wedding cake with a heart on top. Color with pencils.

For the third spread, "The Bird":

1. Using a sponge brush, paint the left-hand page green. Adhere two bird's egg collage images to the left corners.

2. Around the border of the page, draw a vine with leaves in marker and color it in with pencils.

3. Paint the right-hand page and a piece of book board with white acrylic paint. Poke holes in the top and bottom right-hand corners of the board. Poke holes to match in the following two pages and attach the board and pages together with gold brads.

4. Sketch a bird in the right bottom corner of the book board and color it in. For added dimension, cut a branch image, such as from a Cavallini bird print, and glue it to the bird.

Tip

When melting wax to paint, first light a tea candle and wait until the wax is completely melted. Choose a brush that will only be used for wax, dip it into the melted wax and paint the book with the wax. Be careful—the wax will be hot to the touch, but it will also dry quickly. The number of wax layers you apply will determine how visible the images will be. Use a thin layer for a special gloss. A thicker layer gives the images and wording beneath a more mysterious appearance.

For the fourth spread, "The Gown":

1. Paint both pages of the spread in white acrylic paint to match the theme of the dress.

2. Adhere butterfly collage images to the left corners of the left-hand page. Apply rub-on borders to the top, left, and bottom of the page.

3. Paint the right-hand page and a piece of book board with white acrylic paint. Poke holes in the top and bottom right-hand corners of the board. Poke holes to match in the following two pages and attach the board and pages together with gold brads.

4. Use a pencil to draw a wedding gown and veil in the bottom right corner of the book board. Trace over the sketch with a marker and color it in with pencils.

   Note: Excess pages can be removed if not needed.

Tips

- Sketch your drawings in pencil first, so you can make changes, if necessary, before using a marker. Also, tracing over the pencil in marker gives a pleasing effect.

- Think of what you want to include in your book. Remember this is *your* special day—decide what is right for you. Be unique!

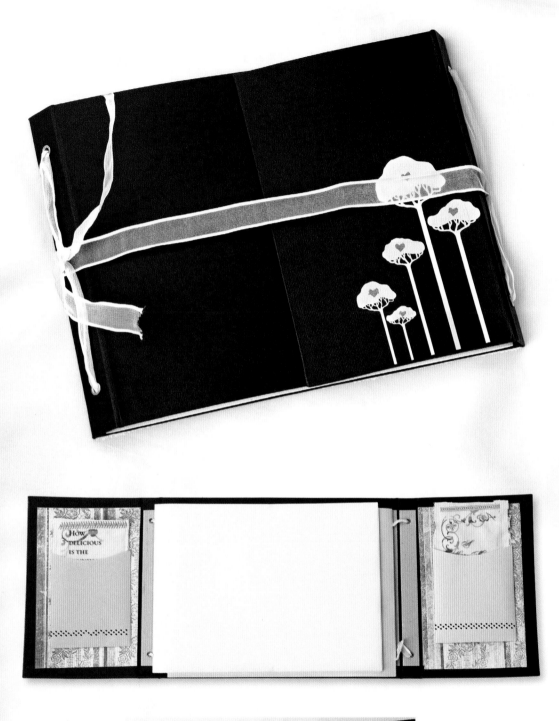

Wedding Journal

Materials

- magnetic gatefold album (10½" x 8" [26.7 x 20.3 cm] shown)
- blue, orange, and brown acrylic paints
- ribbon
- rub-ons
- Cloud 9 Design Series: Photo Banner II Baby Girl
- patterned paper
- pink and purple library pockets
- canvas fabric
- Die Cuts with a View Vellum "Quote Stacks": Wedding & Romance
- brown marker
- Mod Podge
- scissors

Tips

- This is your book. Add motifs that you love, those that inspire you to create and write.
- Feel free to leave some pages blank for words only. It is up to you. Make it your own!

Journaling about the upcoming wedding can help assuage emotions running wild and create an even sturdier bond between the bride and groom. A marriage is a blessing, and sharing your feelings with each other only increases intimacy.

For the cover:

1. Add rub-on trees to the right-hand side of the cover.
2. Apply heart stickers to the trees.
3. For the ribbon tie, cut two pieces of ribbon. On the left-hand side, pull the ribbon (from the inside) through the holes in the side of the album and tie them into a bow.
4. For the right-hand side, pull the ribbon (from the inside) through the two holes. Twist the ribbon and pull one end over the front of the book and one end around to the back. Tie it in a bow in the back.

For the inside front flaps:

1. Adhere patterned paper to each flap.
2. Glue a purple library pocket to the left-hand flap and a pink pocket to the right-hand flap.
3. Add rub-on designs to each pocket.
4. Cut two pieces of canvas fabric to fit the library pockets.
5. Cut out and adhere vellum quotes to fit the canvas pieces.
6. Apply rub-ons to the canvas, placing them to frame the quotes.
7. Adhere the quotes to the canvas with Mod Podge and insert canvas pieces into the pockets.

For the blank pages of the album:

1. With a pencil, sketch vines with small flowers around the page borders. Sketch a flower in the bottom right corner.
2. Outline the sketches in the brown marker, then paint the flowers with blue, orange, and brown acrylic paints.

Pretty Party Book

Materials

- chipboard book (7" x 5" [17.8 x 12.7 cm] shown)
- blue and green acrylic paints
- patterned paper
- collage images of butterflies
- vintage images
- rub-ons
- label holder
- pewter brads
- newsprint paper
- brown marker
- glue
- sponge brush
- scissors
- awl
- glossy photo paper
- computer and printer
- Microsoft Edwardian Script ITC font in bold

Note: Computer-generate the sayings, "Well wishes for the bride and groom …" and "Special memories to share … " and cut them out. The sayings will alternate throughout the inside pages of the book.

Party books are a great way to get the guests involved in the wedding. Guests can write down special memories they have of the couple and add wishes for the days ahead.

For the covers of the book:

1. Cut two pieces of patterned paper to fit the chipboard book. Adhere paper to the front and back covers.

2. Add a rub-on to the bottom right corner of the front cover.

3. Computer-generate the saying "You are my heart" to fit a label holder, cut it out, and adhere it to the center of the cover.

4. With the awl, punch a hole on each side of the saying.

5. Attach the label holder over the label with pewter brads.

For the first spread:

1. Paint the inside cover in green acrylic paint using a sponge brush (see the sidebar on page 37, for more on painting backgrounds). To create a weathered look, remove some of the paint from the brush before painting, so the brush is fairly dry. You might want to have two sponge brushes handy, one for each color, so you do not need to wash the brush with each color change. This will also allow you to work faster.

2. Print out the name of the couple, cut the piece out, and adhere it to the inside cover.

3. Apply a rub-on frame around the names.

4. Add a rub-on to the bottom left corner.

5. Paint the right-hand page in blue acrylic paint using a sponge brush.

6. Adhere the saying "Well wishes for the bride and groom …" to the top of the right-hand page.

7. Apply rub-ons to frame the saying. Add rub-ons randomly around the page.

8. Print a vintage image of a couple, cut it out, and glue to the bottom right corner of the page.

9. Apply a rub-on around it.

For the second spread:

1. With a sponge brush, paint the left-hand page of the spread green and the right-hand page blue. Use the brush to give the pages a weathered look.

2. Add a rub-on to the top of the left-hand page.

3. To the right-hand page, adhere butterfly images, adding faint lines with a marker, to give the impression of flight.

4. Adhere saying "Special memories to share …" to the top of the page and add a rub-on frame. Apply rub-ons randomly around the page.

For the third spread:

1. With a sponge brush, paint the left-hand page of the spread green and the right-hand page blue. Use the brush to give the pages a weathered look.

2. Add a rub-on to the bottom left corner of the left-hand page.

3. Adhere saying "Well wishes for the bride and groom…" to the top of the right-hand page and add a rub-ons to frame the saying. Apply rub-ons randomly around the page.

4. In the bottom right corner, add a vintage image of a flower girl. Apply rub-ons to highlight the flowers with color.

For the fourth spread:

1. With a sponge brush, paint the left-hand page of the spread green and the right-hand page blue. Use the brush to give the pages a weathered look.

2. Add a rub-on to the bottom left corner of the left-hand page.

3. For the right-hand page, adhere the saying "Special memories to share…" to the middle left side of the page and add a rub-on frame.

4. Apply rub-ons randomly around the page.

5. Adhere a collage image to the upper right corner.

Tips

- Make the book fun. Bright colors are a good way to capture your guests' attention.

- Experiment with different phrases for each page.

- Make it personal.

No. 7

Tip

For going sleek, stick to browns, ivories, and creams, as well as muted fall colors.

ELEGANT PARTY BOOK

Materials

- accordion photo album (6" x 8" [15.2 x 20.3 cm] shown)
- thank you rub-ons
- black flower rub-ons
- window envelope
- patterned paper
- glue
- deckle scissors
- computer, paper, and printer

This party book is elegant in its simplicity. It is altered only slightly to suit the bride and groom's desires. Little embellishments can still cause a stir among guests.

For the cover:

1. Print the guest table number (shown "No.7") onto patterned paper. (Note: it might be easier to lightly tape the patterned paper to a sheet of computer paper and run them through the printer.)

2. Cut paper using deckle scissors and adhere it to the book.

3. Apply rub-on flowers to upper left and lower right corners of the book.

For the inside of the book:

1. Apply black flower rub-ons to bottom left corner of each left-hand page.

2. Apply thank you rub-ons to the top right corner of the right-hand pages.

3. At the end of the book, add a window envelope for guests to insert something special.

CHAPTER FOUR

For Others

THE FLOWERS HAVE BEEN CHOSEN, the dress is ready and waiting for the big day. What is left, you ask? Gifts for the wedding party and guests who come to share their congratulations. This chapter explores a variety of gifts togive your bridesmaids, flower girls, your mother, your family and friends. There is something here for everyone; all you need to get started is your creative fingertips!

July 27, 2005

PHOTO KEEPSAKE GIFT

Materials

- bamboo box (4" x 9" [10.2 x 22.9 cm] shown)
- blue acrylic paint
- rub-ons
- bird image
- adhesive foam dots
- patterned paper
- minibirdcage
- bristol board
- wedding photo
- ribbon
- shredded book cloth from a vintage book
- newsprint paper
- sponge brush
- glue
- scissors
- glossy photo paper
- computer and printer
- Microsoft Edwardian Scrip ITC font in bold

Birdcages are often associated with weddings and lovers, in general. Why? Perhaps because birds are seen as gentle creatures, protective and nurturing. Birds are endearing and beautiful, often like love. Birds together in the cage are in their own little world, forever embraced by each other, and such is the message of love through marriage.

For the box:

1. Paint the bamboo box with blue acrylic paint (see the sidebar on page 37, for more on painting backgrounds).
2. Glue patterned paper to the inside bottom of the box.
3. Add rub-ons to the sides and top of the box.
4. Print an image of a bird and attach it to the box, once the cage has been placed using adhesive foam dots and a bit of glue.
5. Tie the ribbon into a bow and attach it to the completed box.

For the cage:

1. Place shredded book cloth from a vintage book cover into the cage.
2. Print an image of the bride and groom and glue it to a small piece of bristol board. Add the couple's names. Paint the edges of the piece.
3. Insert the piece into the cage, setting it into the shredded book cloth.
4. Print the wedding date onto newsprint paper and cut into a tag. Attach it to the cage.
5. Place the cage into the box, then adhere the bird to the box.

Tips

- Instead of using a photo, you can place other items into the birdcage. Tuck in a special note, for example, that only the recipient will see.

- This can also be a great gift from the bride to groom and vice versa!

BRIDESMAID BOX

Materials

- round shaker box (6"d x 4"h [15.2 x 10.2 cm] shown)
- pink and white acrylic paints
- tag
- bird image
- excelsior or raffia to fill box, such as Wonder Wood
- vintage fabric leaves
- ribbon
- safety pin
- sponge brush
- fan brush
- glue
- scissors
- glossy photo paper
- computer and printer

Every bridesmaid is unique. To show that she is meaningful to you, give her a gift as special as she is. Gifts that express your gratitude to those intimately involved in the experience of your wedding day can be difficult to find. A box can hold a variety of items: tiny trinkets, a book of thanks, or memories of the special day.

For the box:

1. Using a sponge brush, paint the base of a shaker box in white acrylic paint and the lid in pink (see the sidebar on page 37, for more on painting backgrounds).

2. Add excelsior, such as Wonder Wood, to the inside.

3. Glue one end of a piece of ribbon to the bottom of the box and wrap it around the box, so the ends meet.

4. Glue a second piece of ribbon to the bottom and wrap it around the box the opposite way (as if you were wrapping a gift). Connect the two ribbons at the bottom with a safety pin.

5. Print an image of a bluebird and glue it to a small tag. Give the tag a weathered look by painting the edges with a fan brush in white acrylic paint.

6. Add leaves to the ribbon and tie the tag to them on top of the box.

THE BOOK (ACCOMPANYING PIECE)

Materials

- chipboard minibook (3" x 3" [7.6 x 7.6 cm] shown)
- blue and white acrylic paints
- rub-ons
- images
- black marker
- red pencil
- drawing pencil
- tassel
- sponge brush
- glue
- scissors
- awl
- glossy photo paper
- computer and printer

For the covers:

1. Using a sponge brush, paint the front and back covers with blue acrylic paint (see the sidebar on page 37, for more on painting backgrounds).

2. Add a birdcage rub-on to the front cover. Draw a small heart in the corner with a red-colored pencil and outline it in black marker.

3. With the awl, punch a hole near the top of the book's spine and pull a tassel through. Add glue to keep it in place.

Tip

Instead of using generic images, include images of your friend as a child to make the book more meaningful.

For the first spread:

1. Using a sponge brush, paint both pages in the spread with blue and white acrylic paint. Note: Do this for all the remaining spreads, except the last spread.

2. Apply rub-ons to the left-hand page.

3. Adhere a vintage photo (or a photo of the bridesmaid as a child) to the right-hand page.

4. Draw wings on the photo and sketch a frame around the image.

5. Above the image, print the words "You have been there from the start" with a black marker.

THE BOOK (CONTINUED)

For the second spread:

1. On the left-hand page, print the phrase "through the joy" with a black marker. Apply a design rub-on beneath the phrase.

2. Adhere a vintage image of a woman to the right-hand page. Sketch the hand in pencil and apply a rub-on bird.

For the third spread:

1. To the left-hand page, adhere a vintage image of a woman crying and apply rub-ons.

2. Print the phrase "through the tears" on the right-hand page with a black marker. Apply rub-ons to the bottom left corner.

For the fourth spread:

1. Print or photocopy images of hands. Adhere them to the center of the spread, so that they connect. Print the phrase "you have held my hand" across the top of both pages with a black marker.

2. Add rub-ons to the bottom of both pages.

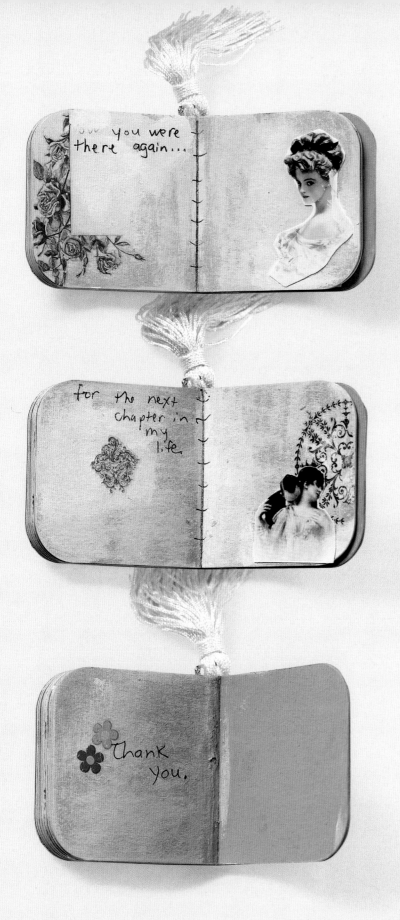

For the fifth spread:

1. Apply a rub-on to the left-hand page. Print the phrase "You were there again …" on the page with a black marker.

2. Adhere a vintage image of a bridesmaid to the right-hand page.

For the sixth spread:

1. Print the phrase "for the next chapter in my life" on the left-hand page with a black marker and add a rub-on.

2. Apply a rub-on to the right-hand page, then adhere an image of a couple over the rub-on.

For the final spread:

1. Paint only the left-hand page with blue and white acrylic paint.

2. Print the words "thank you" with a black marker and add flower rub-ons.

ENDEARING BRIDESMAID BOX WITH NECKLACE

Materials

- organza box with ribbon (6" x 6" [15.2 x 15.2 cm] box shown)
- patterned paper
- illustration board
- bird image
- vintage fabric daisies (ivory)
- excelsior or raffia, such as Wonder Wood, to fill the box
- scissors
- glossy photo paper
- glue (if necessary)
- computer and printer

For bridesmaids who fancy jewelry, this little box and necklace (shown on page 88) is the perfect thank-you gift. The box is simple, elegant, and holds something more precious than anything: an expression of what it means to be a friend.

For the box:

1. Cut paper to fit the sides, cover, and bottom of the box. Note: cut two of the side pieces half the height of the box, to create windows. Adhere the paper to the inside of the box.

2. Add excelsior or raffia, such as Wonder Wood.

3. Tie the wire stem of the flowers around the ribbon on the lid of the box.

4. Print a bird image onto paper, cut it out, and glue it to a piece of illustration board. Cut the bird from the board and make a stand for it. (Cut a piece of illustration board into a semicircle, then cut a slit in it. Cut a small slit in the feet of the bird.)

5. Slide the bird into the stand and slide the stand under the ribbon.

THE NECKLACE

Materials

- charm (1.5"h [3.8 cm] shown)
- chain necklace
- clip
- bead
- leaf charm clip
- the word "dream," cut from an old book
- Diamond Glaze
- scissors
- glossy photo paper
- computer and printer
- image of a fairy

The pendant is made by adding a simple collage to a blank charm. Customize each one to make them unique.

For the necklace:

1. Cut a piece of patterned paper and glue it to a blank charm.

2. Add an image of a fairy and the word "dream."

3. Apply Diamond Glaze over the collage image and let it dry overnight.

4. Attach the completed collage charm, the leaf charm, and a bead to a chain.

Tip

Choose images and sayings that suit the personality of the person receiving it. A great place for vintage images is Enchanted Mercantile Vintage Graphics (see Resources, page 110, for more information).

Box and Canvas Heart Pocket with Necklace for Maid of Honor

Materials

- wood pencil box (3" x 8" [7.6 x 20.3 cm] shown)
- orange acrylic paint
- patterned paper
- rub-ons
- excelsior or raffia, such as Wonder Wood, to fill the box
- flower seeds
- glue
- scissors
- deckle scissors

(necklace materials list on page 93)

The maid of honor is that special person chosen to aid the bride in her tasks both before and on the day of the wedding. She is the one who sees the bride through much of her turmoil and joy. Giving a gift made from the heart is one of the best ways to thank the friend who was there through it all. This page features the gift box. The necklace and heart pocket are shown on page 92.

For the box:

1. Paint the inside and outside of the pencil box with orange acrylic paint (see the sidebar on page 37, for more on painting).

2. Glue patterned paper to the top edges and ends of the box (as pictured). Glue two narrow strips along the top of the long sides of the box.

3. Cut two strips of patterned paper with deckle scissors and adhere the strips along the bottom of each long side of the box.

4. Apply rub-ons to the long sides and the lid of the box.

5. Add excelsior or raffia, such as Wonder Wood, to the inside of the box along with some sprinkled flower seeds.

6. Place the completed necklace (instructions follow) into the box.

Tip

Adding some natural deco-
rations, such as flower seeds
or dried flowers, to the
inside of the gift box is a
great touch.

MAID OF HONOR NECKLACE

Materials

- canvas fabric
- ribbon
- fold-over leaf finding
- swivel charm (2" [5.1 cm] shown)
- gold chain
- patterned paper
- wedding image
- newsprint paper
- needle and thread
- glue
- scissors
- glossy photo paper
- computer and printer
- Microsoft Times New Roman font in bold and italics

This necklace is just one gift suggestion for the maid of honor. Feel free to substitute a gift that suits the receiver's preference.

For the heart:

1. Cut four heart shapes from canvas fabric.

2. Cut a heart shape from patterned paper to fit the canvas heart.

3. Sew the canvas heart to the paper heart.

4. Sew the paper-canvas heart to another canvas heart.

5. Sew the remaining two canvas hearts together. (You should have two hearts.) Sew the two heart sets together around the "V" to make a pocket.

For the necklace:

1. Cut and glue a piece of patterned paper to each side of the charm.

2. Print a small image from the wedding and glue it to the charm.

3. On the opposite side of the charm, adhere the saying "Thank you for being my friend."

4. Add the charm to a necklace chain, then slip the charm into the canvas heart pocket.

5. Tie a small piece of ribbon around the heart.

6. Use a fold-over leaf finding to clasp the ribbon in place.

HEART-SHAPED FLOWER GIRL GIFT

Materials

- organza heart-shaped box (4"d x 1½"h [10.2 x 3.8 cm] shown)
- vintage forget-me-nots garland
- vintage flowers (light lilac nosegays)
- plastic heart
- patterned paper
- oval frame finding
- rub-on
- photo
- vintage music paper image
- wire
- glue
- scissors

Flower girls play an important role in the bridal party, and they deserve something just as beautiful as they are. This small, simple box is a great place for a little girl to hold treasures from that special day, as well as the secrets of her heart as she grows older.

For the box:

1. Cut patterned paper to size and glue it to the inside top and bottom of the heart-shaped box.

2. Attach a flower garland around the outside of the box. Use wire, if necessary.

3. Adhere a plastic heart to the center of the box lid. Add a vintage flower.

4. Apply a rub-on and a photo of the flower girl to the inside bottom of the box. Adhere a small frame finding over the photo.

5. Adhere two vintage flowers and a sheet music image to the inside top of the box.

Tips

- Cut the paper to fit the box, then slide it into the wire of the organza box.

- If you do not have a photo of the flower girl, use a vintage photo, perhaps from the family or from a collage sheet.

FLOWER GIRL THANK-YOU BOX

Materials

- blank box (6"d [15.2 cm] square box shown)
- patterned paper
- card stock
- library pocket
- ribbon
- rub-ons
- white acrylic paint
- Cloud 9 Design Series: Photo Banner II Baby Girl
- oval label, such as Martha Stewart
- vintage leaves
- Spanish moss
- fan brush
- utility knife
- glue
- scissors
- glossy photo paper
- computer and printer

Give the youngest member of the bridal party a place to keep her treasured memories for years to come. This special box can hold dried flowers, a thank-you note, or a special memento, such as photos of the moments leading up to the wedding.

The box:

1. Adhere patterned paper to the sides and the top of the box. Excess paper can be trimmed with a utility knife.
2. Adhere coordinating paper to the rim of the lid.
3. Adhere a piece of ribbon around the lid of the box.
4. Cut another piece of ribbon to tie a bow around the completed box.
5. Adhere patterned paper to the inside of the lid and place Spanish moss inside the box.

For the card and pocket:

1. Adhere a Martha Stewart oval label and a thank-you rub-on to the front of the library pocket.
2. Cut a piece of card stock (or the coordinating paper) to fit inside the pocket. Apply rub-ons to the corners of the card.
3. Print a photo of the flower girl and glue it to the card. Paint the edges with white acrylic paint using a fan brush.
4. Apply stickers to the top and bottom of the photo. Adhere a vintage leaf sprig to the corner.

Tips

- Add flower seeds to the Spanish moss for a bit of color.
- Instead of Spanish moss, layer the box with dried flowers from the wedding and tuck in a personal thank-you note.

WEDDING FRAME

Materials

- magnet frame (3¾" x 3¼" [9.5 x 8.3 cm] purple frame shown)
- rub-ons
- collage sheet image
- white marker
- image of the couple
- glue
- scissors
- computer paper
- glossy photo paper
- computer and printer

Images from the wedding, reception, or even intimate portraits from the couple can be a wonderful reminder of friendships and moments when people come together as one. Small magnet frames are one way to do just that.

For the inside of the frame:

1. Cut a piece of computer paper to fit the inside measurements of the frame. (Use the frame backing to determine the correct size.)

2. Adhere a collage image to the paper.

3. Cut out a favorite photo of the couple and adhere it over the collage image.

For the frame:

1. Add rub-ons to the corners and one side of the frame.

2. Use a white marker to add the wedding date.

3. Insert the photo into the frame.

Tips

- A framed photo is an inexpensive way to say thank you to your guests. Instead of using rub-ons, try sketching flowers and flourishes. Draw the sketch in pencil first, if you like.

- Instead of using a wedding photo, choose an engagement photo or a photo that holds meaning for you and that you want to share with friends and family.

THANK YOU

Tips

- Instead of a thank you, write a special message for the guest's eyes only.

- As an alternative, adhere an image in the window section of the box.

MONOGRAMMED WEDDING BOX FRAME

Materials

- 3 ½" x 3 ½" x 2" small chipboard box with a window (3 ½" [8.9 cm] square box, shown)
- white and gray acrylic paints
- patterned paper
- rub-ons
- gold letter rub-on
- thank-you rub-on
- adhesive label
- fold-over leaf finding
- bristol board
- image of the couple
- ribbon
- glue
- scissors
- glossy photo paper
- computer and printer

Create this small box as an alternative to the usual picture frame. Inside its secret door, the box holds the couple's photo and a message of thanks. It is a creative way to give thanks to the guests who shared your day (and to show off your new wedding photos).

For the box:

1. Paint the inside and outside of the box, except the spine, with white acrylic paint (see the sidebar on page 37, for more on painting backgrounds). Paint the spine gray and let dry. Apply a decorative rub-on letter (I used the first letter of the couple's last name: R) to the top of the box.

2. Cut a paper heart from patterned paper and glue it to the spine of the box. Add rub-ons to the top and bottom of the spine.

3. Apply a thank-you rub-on to an adhesive label. Adhere the label to the inside bottom of the box.

4. Print an image of the wedding couple, cut it out, and glue it to bristol board for extra strength.

5. Carefully fold the image in half and use a fold-over leaf to hold it closed.

6. Tie a ribbon around the photo.

7. Place the photo into the box.

Mark and Tammy
August 21, 2007

CHERISHED SHADOW BOX

Materials

- shadow box (6" x 8" [15.2 x 20.3 cm] shown)
- pink acrylic paint
- decorative rub-on
- personal photos and/or collage sheet images
- adhesive foam board
- vintage flowers
- vintage tacks
- label holder
- newsprint paper
- double-sided permanent tape
- scissors
- glue
- glossy photo paper
- computer and printer

A shadow box frame is an inexpensive and novel way to display favorite images for family and friends and makes a lovely gift!

For the box:

1. Paint the shadow box with pink acrylic paint (see the sidebar on page 37 for more information).

2. Adhere a decorative rub-on to the top left corner.

3. Create a label by printing the couple's name and wedding date onto newsprint paper and cutting it out.

4. Glue the label to the shadowbox. Attach a label holder over the label with vintage tacks.

For the images:

1. Print a photo of a wedding couple. Cut out the photo and adhere it with double-sided tape to a piece of foam board. Trim the foam board around the image.

2. Print a background image for the photo or cut one from a collage sheet. Size the image to fit the cardboard insert from the shadow box. Adhere the background image to the insert. Ensure that the background image completely covers the insert.

3. Peel the paper from the back of the adhesive foam board and adhere the photo to the background image.

4. Insert the completed piece into the frame.

5. Glue vintage flowers to the glass.

Tips

- A shadow box photo is a wonderful gift for the parents of the bride and groom. This shadow box is an innovative frame for precious photos and is also a unique way to share memories of the wedding day.

- Instead of using collage images for the background, use a photo that otherwise might have been overlooked. Including personal images from a special time in your life, along with photos from your wedding day, makes the gift even more meaningful.

MOTHER-OF-THE-BRIDE KEEPSAKE

Materials

- chipboard box with lid (3" x 3" [7.6 x 7.6 cm] shown)
- patterned papers
- illustration board
- photo of couple
- vintage paper leaves
- button
- linen thread or embroidery floss
- twigs
- newsprint paper
- ribbon
- utility knife
- glue
- scissors
- awl
- glossy photo paper
- computer and printer

Our mothers are with us for the long haul, sharing our joys, offering wanted (and unwanted!) advice, and always providing enduring support.

For the box:

1. Adhere patterned paper to the inside and outside of the chipboard box. Cut any excess paper with a utility knife.

2. Print a photo of the wedding couple onto photo paper and glue it to illustration board. Trim around the image. Adhere a piece of patterned paper to the back of the image and glue the photo to the top of the box.

3. Glue the leaves to the top of the box, next to the picture.

4. Adhere a button to the front of the box.

5. Punch a hole into the lid of the box and tie a piece of linen thread through it, knotting it several times. Be sure to cut the thread long enough to wrap around the button for closure.

For the inside:

1. Add a nest of twigs to the inside of the box.

2. Write or print a special message for the mother of the bride on newsprint paper.

3. To give the message a worn look, tear off the ends and it roll up.

4. Tie a ribbon around the note. Cut a heart from patterned paper and glue it to the ribbon.

PRODUCT MANUFACTURERS BY PROJECT

Page18
Our History Accordion Book

Accordion book (Bazzill Basics Paper, Inc.: Accordion Keeper: Cottowood); colored cardstock (Bazzill Basics Paper Inc.: Earthtone); collage image (Enchanted Mercantile Vintage Graphics CD: *Vintage Ephemera, Volume One*);decorative buttons (Dill Buttons); wedding couple image (ARTchix Studio: Marry Me collage sheet); Grafix Rub-Onz transfer film; rub-ons (Karen Foster Design Wedding Rub-Bits; American Crafts miniMARKS: Accents, Books One and Three; Fancy Pants Designs: French Market); patterned paper (Basic Grey Lilykate: Bamboo); brown and black markers (Sakura, Pigma Micron 05); Prismacolor pencil by Sanford (Sienna Brown and Black); charm (Frost Creek Charms); Victorian Scrap (Victorian Scrapworks); glue (Scotch 3M); Kodak Gloss Photo Paper; Microsoft Bradley Hand ITC font in bold.

Page 22
Blushing Bride's Diary

Westrim Paper Bliss 3-D Board Book, Rectangle; Folk Art acrylic paint (Plaid Enterprises, Inc.: #427 Mushroom); brown marker (Sakura, Pigma Micron 05); pencils (Faber Castell); colored pencil (Prismacolor by Sanford: Crimson Red), white pastel pencil (Rexel Derwent) rub-ons (Fancy Pants Designs: Cherish); alphabet letter transfers (Martha Stewart Crafts, manufactured by EK Success: White Chisel Type Transfers); Computer Grafix clear adhesive inkjet film, glue (Scotch 3M); deckle scissors (Anita's Arts); template, page 23.

Page 26
Keepsake Wedding Album

Folk Art acrylic paint (Plaid Enterprises, Inc.: #920 Autumn Leaves, #430 Spring White, #438 Ballet Pink, #425 Medium Gray, #467 Italian Sage, #959 English Mustard, #318 Passion Punch, #901 Wicker White, #753 Rose Chiffon, #639 French Blue); vintage cabinet card photo album (eBay); images (Enchanted Mercantile Vintage Graphics CDs: *Victorian Ephemera* and *Vintage Ephemera, Volume One*); rubber stamps (quote on the cover: Catslife Press; quote inside: Stamping Sensations); rub-ons (American Crafts miniMARKS: Accents, Books One, Three, and Four; My Mind's Eye Bohemia: Darling); Die Cuts With a View Vellum "Quote Stacks": Wedding & Romance; ribbon (Nicole Crafts); patterned papers (Me and My Big Ideas: La Jolla; My Mind's Eye Wild Asparagus: Pink Floral; K&Company: Ashford Floral Stripe; Cosmo Cricket Wanted Collection: Doc Holiday, Kissin Kate; Storytime Collection: Jumping Joan; Cosmo Cricket Love Notes Collection: Together Again; Fancy Pants Designs fancy-free collection Free Spirit: Victorian Lace; Cavallini Papers & Company, Inc.: Bird & Nest Decorative Wrap; newsprint paper (Pro Art), collage sheets (ARTchix Studio: Door to Door); Kisses collage sheet (Tallulah's Art); antique gold label holder and mini pewter brads (Making Memories); brown marker (Sakura, Pigma Micron 05); adhesive foam dots (Mini Pop Dots, All Night Media); glue (Scotch 3M); Kodak Ultra Premium High Gloss Photo Paper; Tim Holtz Distress Ink: Vintage Photo (Ranger).

Page 32
Honeymoon Journal

Blank scrapbook (Made For Retail, Inc.); patterned paper (My Mind's Eye Signature Suite by Jen Wilson: Little Girls are ..., Sweet Dots, Bare White); Folk Art acrylic paint (Plaid Enterprises, Inc. #901 Wicker White and #433 Terra Cotta); rub-ons (Fancy Pants: French Market, Cherish and Mulberry Road; My Mind's Eye Bohemia, Blossom: Darling; American Crafts miniMARKS: Accents, Books One, Two, and Four; Chatterbox, Inc. Grafik Rub-Ons: Borders: Black and White); images (Enchanted Mercantile Vintage Graphics CDs: *Vintage Scraps, Vintage Ephemera, Volume Two* and *Vintage Ephemera, Volume One*; Red Letter Art, LLC: Collage Images CD #1); brown and black markers (Sakura, Pigma Micron 05 and 08); Die Cuts With a View Vellum "Quote Stacks": Wedding & Romance; adhesive foam dots (Mini Pop Dots, All Night Media); ribbon (Fancy Pants Designs: fancy-free collection: Free Spirit) Prismacolor pencil by Sanford (Light Cerulean Blue); library pocket (Bazzill Basics Paper, Inc.: Wisteria); Computer Grafix clear adhesive inkjet film.

Page 38
Mini brag book

Mini album (Bazzill Basics Paper, Inc. mono mini album: Jacaranda); pressed flowers (Pressed Petals); collage image (Altered Pages: color ATC collage sheet as a transparency); rub-ons (Fancy Pants Designs: Mulberrry Road); patterned paper (Cosmo Cricket Storytime Collection: Jumping Joan), Prismacolor pencil by Sanford (Crimson Red); newsprint paper (Pro Art); glue (Scotch 3M); Kodak Gloss Photo Paper.

Page 42
Altered Dream Journal
Westrim Paper Bliss 3-D Board Book Square, Folk Art acrylic paint (Plaid Enterprises, Inc.: #642 Blue Ink, #430 Spring White, #433 Terra Cotta, #637 Orchid, and #467 Italian Sage); images (Enchanted Mercantile Vintage Graphics CD: *Victorian Ephemera and Vintage Scraps*, *Vintage Ephemera, Volume Two*; Tallulah's Art: Wings download and Playful download); rustic primitive heart (Provo Craft); Galaxy Milky Way White Marker (American Crafts);mini pewter brads and pewter label holder (Making Memories); dollhouse gothic window (Grandt Line); leaf charm (Blue Moon Beads, a Division of Creativity, Inc.); rub-ons (Martha Stewart Crafts, manufactured by EK Success: Black Ornata Alphabet Letter Transfers; Fancy Pants Designs: Elegance; American Crafts miniMARKS: Accents, Book Three; 7 gypsies Rubbings Elements: Whimsy copyrights belong to Ultra-PRO); patterned paper (Daisy D's: Charles River; Fancy Pants Designs fancy-free collection Wildheart: Stained Stripes, Dreamer; My Mind's Eye Signature Life by Jen Wilson: Everyday "Love" Heart Imprints/Tickled Pink Paper); collage sheet image (Tomorrow's Unknown #183); library pocket (Bazzill Basics Paper, Inc.); pastel pencils (Rexel Derwent: Geranium Lake; Orange Earth, Deep Cadmium); drawing pencils (Rexel Derwent); quote (European Papers: Romance Quotes #1); newsprint paper (Pro Art); blue marker (Sakura, Pigma 05) glue (Scotch 3M); Kodak Ultra Premium High Gloss Photo Paper; Computer Grafix clear adhesive inkjet film.

Page 46
Handbound Dream Journal
Heavy chipboard (Paper Accents by Accent Design); book cloth (Quiet Fire Design & Lettering Art); paper (Bazzill Basics Paper, Inc.: Earthtone); ribbon (Nicole Crafts); rub-on (Fancy Pants Designs: French Market); patterned paper (Fancy Pants Designs Fancy Aged Florals Papers: Love Bird); Paper Mod Podge (Plaid Enterprises, Inc.).

Page 48
The Nest Journal
Small vintage cabinet card photo album (eBay); Folk Art acrylic paint (Plaid Enterprises, Inc.: #901 Wicker White, #465 Sky Blue, and #959 English Mustard); ribbon (Nicole Crafts); images (Enchanted Mercantile Vintage Graphics CDs: *Vintage Ephemera, Volume One*; *Vintage Scraps*; *Vintage Ephemera, Volume Two*; Tallulah's Art: Intimate download, Kiss download, Love download); rub-ons (American Crafts miniMARKS: Accents, Books One, Three, and Four); Die Cuts With a View Vellum Quote Stack: Wedding & Romance; patterned paper (Cosmo Cricket Love Notes Collection : Darling); glue (Scotch 3M); Kodak Ultra Premium High Gloss Photo Paper.

Page 56
Bridal Planner
Accordion pocket portfolio-Persimmon (Martha Stewart Crafts, manufactured by EK Success); Embossed Heirloom Window Pocket Cards (Martha Stewart Crafts, manufactured by EK Success); Black Ornata Alphabet Letter K transfer (Martha Stewart Crafts, manufactured by EK Success); rub-ons (Fancy Pants Designs: Truly, Madly, Deeply); glue (Scotch 3M).

Page 56
Bridal Planner Interior Page
Cardstock (Bazzill Basics Paper, Inc.: Earthtone), Basic Grey patterned paper (Periphery: Cabernet, and Aged & Confused Sublime Collection: Lemonade); collage images (Enchanted Mercantile Vintage Graphics CD: Vintage Scraps, Vintage Ephemera Volume Two, and Red Letter Art, LLC.; Collage Images CD #1 [Note one image has been altered with text using Adobe Photoshop CS]); Pewter brads and label holder (Making Memories), rub-ons: Basic Grey: Lost Boys (White), Euro Edge (White); American Crafts miniMARKS accents, book one); small gold photo turns (7 gypsies copyrights belong to Ultra-PRO); clip (7 gypsies Zanzibar Collection copyrights beong to Ultra-PRO); black marker (Sakura, Pigma Micron 05).

Page 58
Pocket Planner
ring rub-on (Karen Foster Design: Wedding Rub-Bits); rub-ons (American Crafts: Accents Book Three); Grafix Rub-Onz transfer film; Bristol board (Strathmore); Folk Art acrylic paint (Plaid Enterprises, Inc.: #442 Baby Blue, #450 Parchment, #425 Medium Gray); collage image (Altered Pages: Awesome Archways AP-890); black marker (Sakura, Pigma Micron 08); Paper Reflections Creative Tags (DMD Industries, Inc.); patterned paper (Basic Grey Periphery: Cabernet) glue (Scotch 3M).

Page 62
Wedding Guest Book
Folk Art acrylic paint (Plaid Enterprises, Inc.: #438 Ballet Pink, #901

Wicker White, #645 Basil Green, #909 Bluebell); Prismacolor pencils by Sanford (Apple Green, Lilac, Crimson Red, Light Cerulean Blue, Yellowed Orange, Light Umber); brown fine-point marker (Sakura, Pigma Micron 05); images (Cavallini Papers & Co., Inc.: Bird & Nest Decorative Wrap; Altered Pages: artist collage sheet Tag Collage AP-870); rub-ons (American Crafts miniMARKS: Accents, Books Three and Four); patterned paper (Cosmo Cricket Love Notes Collection: Darling); flower embellishments (EK Success: Jolee's Boutique-Jolee's By You: Purple Gerbera); adhesive foam dots (Mini Pop Dots, All Night Media); ribbon (Morex Corp.);buttons (Blumenthal Lansing Co.: la petite); glue (Scotch 3M).

Page 68
Wedding Journal
Album (Bazzill Basics Paper, Inc. Gatefold: Raven); Folk Art acrylic paint (Plaid Enterprises, Inc.: #433 Terra Cotta, #427 Mushroom, #465 Sky Blue); ribbon (Morex Corp.); rub-ons (Hambly Studios (Mod Trees); Chatterbox Inc. Grafik Rub-Ons Borders: Black and White; Fancy Pants Designs: Elegance); self adhesive 3-D gel stitches (Cloud 9 Design Series Photo Banner II: Baby Girl); patterned paper (Fancy Pants Designs fancy-free collection, Wildheart: Stained Stripes); library envelopes in pink and purple (Bazzill Basics Paper, Inc.: Romance and Wisteria); Die Cuts With a View Vellum "Quote Stacks": Wedding & Romance; brown marker (Sakura, Pigma Micron 05); Paper Mod Podge (Plaid Enterprises, Inc).

Page 70
Pretty Party Book
Chipboard book (Maya Road: Dinner Break); Folk Art acrylic paint (Plaid Enterprises, Inc.: #465 Sky Blue, #645 Basil Green); patterned paper (Daisy D's: Boston Flourish); butterflies (Cavallini Papers & Company, Inc: Bird & Nest Decorative Wrap.); vintage images (Enchanted Mercantile Vintage Graphics CDs: *Vintage Scraps, Vintage Ephemera, Volume Two,* and *Vintage Ephemera, Volume One*; Tallulah's Art: Kiss Download); rub-ons (Fancy Pants Designs Cherish: Aged Floral and Truly, Madly, Deeply; American Crafts miniMARKS: Accents, Book One, Three, and Four); pewter label holder and mini pewter brads (Making Memories); newsprint paper (Pro Art); brown marker (Sakura, Pigma Micron 05); glue (Scotch 3M); Kodak Ultra Premium High Gloss Photo Paper; Microsoft Edwardian Script ITC font in bold.

Page 74
Elegant Party Book
Walnut Accordion album (Martha Stewart Crafts, manufactured by EK Success); framed thank you transfers and flower transfers (Martha Stewart Crafts, manufactured by EK Success); black flower rub-ons (American Crafts miniMARKS: Accents, Book Two); Embossed Heirloom Window Pocket Cards (Martha Stewart Crafts, manufactured by EK Success); patterned paper (Fancy Pants Designs fancy-free collection Free Spirit: Victorian Lace); glue (Scotch 3M); deckle scissors (Anita's Arts); Microsoft Word Garamond font in bold.

Page 78
Photo Keepsake Gift
Folk Art acrylic paint (Plaid Enterprises, Inc.: #909 Bluebell); rub-ons (American Crafts miniMARKS: Accents, Book One); bird image (Enchanted Mercantile Vintage Graphics CD: *Victorian Ephemera*); adhesive foam dots (Mini Pop Dots All Night Media); patterned paper (Me and My Big Ideas: Venice); bristol board (Strathmore); newsprint paper (Pro Art); glue (Scotch 3M); Kodak Ultra Premium High Gloss Photo Paper; Microsoft Edwardian Script ITC font in bold.

Page 80
Bridesmaid Box
Round Shaker box (Nicole Crafts); Folk Art acrylic paint (Plaid Enterprises, Inc.: #430 Spring White, #438 Ballet Pink, #909 Bluebell); bird image (Enchanted Mercantile Vintage Graphics CD: *Victorian Ephemera*); Wonder Wood, Rocky Mountain Aspen (excelsior); leaves (Modern Romance, Hirschberg Schutz & Co); ribbon (Morex Corp); brown marker (Sakura, Pigma Micron 05); glue (Scotch 3M); Kodak Ultra Premium High Gloss Photo Paper; Paper Reflections Creative Tags (DMD Industries, Inc.) chipboard minibook (Maya Road Memento Collection: secret box); rub-ons (Hambly Studios: Out on a Limb; Fancy Pants Designs: Aged Floral); Prismacolor pencil by Sanford (Poppy); tassel (Wrights,) images (Enchanted Mercantile Vintage Graphics CDs: *Vintage Scraps, Vintage Ephemera, Volume Two* and *Victorian Ephemera*; Tallulah's Art collage sheets and downloads: Kisses, 20 Beauties, and Mandel).

Page 86
Endearing Bridesmaid Box with Necklace
Organza box (All in the Cards Inc.); patterned paper (Cosmo Cricket Love Notes Collection: Darling); bird image (Enchanted Mercantile Vintage Graphics CD: Victorian Ephemera); Wonder Wood, Rocky Mountain Aspen (excelsior); necklace, clip, bead and leaf charm (Blue Moon Beads, A Division of Creativity, Inc.); Diamond Glaze (Judikins); Kodak Ultra Premium High Gloss Photo Paper.

Page 90
Box and Canvas Heart Pocket with Necklace for Maid of Honor
Pencil box (Nicole Crafts); Folk Art acrylic paint (Plaid Enterprises, Inc.: #433 Terra Cotta); patterned paper (My Mind's Eye, Christmas: "Believe" Paisley Paper; Fancy Pants Designs fancy-free collection Free Spirit: Victorian Lace); Wonder Wood, Rocky Mountain Aspen (excelsior), rub-ons (Fancy Pants Designs: Clair de Lune), deckle scissors (Anita's Arts); Ribbon (Nicole Crafts); newsprint paper (Pro Art); glue (Scotch 3M); Microsoft Times Roman font in bold and italics.

Page 94
Heart-Shaped Flower Girl Gift
Organza heart-shaped box (All in the Cards, Inc.); plastic heart (Jesse James Beads: Dress it Up); patterned paper (Cosmo Cricket Storytime Collection: Pixie Dust); rub-ons (American Crafts miniMARKS: Accents, Book Three); music paper (Enchanted Mercantile Vintage Graphics CD: *Vintage Scraps, Vintage Ephemera, Volume Two*) glue (Scotch 3M).

Page 96
Flower Girl Thank-You Box
Blank box (A.C. Moore, Inc.); patterned paper (My Mind's Eye Signature Life Collection by Jen Wilson: Everyday Love: Heart Imprints/ Tickled Pink); Folk Art acrylic paint (Plaid Enterprises, Inc.: #901 Wicker White); library pocket (Bazzill Basics Paper, Inc: Romance); ribbon (Offray); rub-ons (Chatterbox Inc. Grafik Rub-on Borders: Butter/Tangerine; Martha Stewart Crafts, manufactured by EK Success: framed thank-you transfers); self adhesive 3-D gel stitches (Cloud 9 Design Series Photo Banner II: Baby Girl); oval flourish label (Martha Stewart Crafts, manufactured by EK Success); glue (Scotch 3M); Kodak Gloss Photo Paper.

Page 98
Wedding Frame
Magnet frame (Bazzill Basics Paper, Inc.: Heidi); rub-ons (American Craft miniMARKS: Accents, Book Three); Galaxy Milky Way White marker (American Crafts); glue (Scotch 3M).

Page 100
Monogrammed Wedding Box Frame
Small chipboard box (Maya Road Memento Collection); Folk Art acrylic paint (Plaid Enterprises, Inc.: #428 Rose White and #936 Barn Wood); patterned paper (Fancy Pants Designs fancy–free collection Free Spirit: Victorian Lace); rub-ons (Fancy Pants Designs: Aged Floral); ribbon (Fancy Pants Designs); gold letter monogram transfer (Martha Stewart Crafts, manufactured by EK Success);framed thank-you transfer and oval flourish label (Martha Stewart Crafts, manufactured by EK Success); bristol board (Strathmore); glue (Scotch 3M); Kodak Ultra Premium High Gloss Photo Paper.

Page 102
Cherished Shadow Box
Folk Art acrylic paint (Plaid Enterprises, Inc.: #318 Passion Punch); rub-on (Fancy Pants Designs: Mulberry Road); background photo (can be purchased from Altered Pages in a smaller form, from artist's collage sheet Snow and Ice AP-822); pewter label holder (Making Memories); newsprint paper (Pro Art); permanent double-sided tape and glue (Scotch 3M); self-adhesive foam board (Elmer's); Kodak Gloss Photo Paper.

Page 104
Mother-of-the-Bride Keepsake
Keepsake cube (Maya Road Memento Collection); patterned papers (My Mind's Eye Signature Suite by Jen Wilson: Aged Floral, Soft Sienna, Little Girls Are …; Fancy Pants Designs fancy-free collection Free Spirit: Victorian Lace); button (Blumenthal Lansing Co: la petite); newsprint paper (Pro Art); ribbon (Fancy Pants Designs fancy-free collection: Free Spirit); glue (Scotch 3M); Kodak High Gloss Photo Paper.

RESOURCES

Adhesives, Paints, Mediums, Pencils and Markers

3M
www.3m.com

Anita's Arts
www.anitasarts.com

Derwent
www.pencils.co.uk

Elmer's
www.elmers.com

Faber-Castell USA
www.faber-castell.us

Golden Artist Colors, Inc.
www.goldenpaints.com

Judikins
www.judikins.com

Liquitex
www.liquitex.com

Plaid Enterprises, Inc.
www.plaidenterprises.com

Prismacolor
www.prismacolor.com

Sakura of America
www.gellyroll.com

Patterned Paper and Paper Products

Basic Grey
www.basicgrey.com

Bazzill Basics
www.bazzillbasics.com

Cavallini Papers & Co., Inc.
www.cavallini.com

Cosmo Cricket
www.cosmocricket.com

Daisy D's
www.daisyds.com

European Papers
www.europeanpapers.com

Fancy Pants Designs
www.fancypantsdesigns.com

Grafix
www.grafixarts.com

Hannah Grey Curiosities & Drygoods
www.hannahgrey.com

K&Company
www.kandcompany.com

Kodak photo paper
www.kodak.com

Maya Road
www.mayaroad.com

My Mind's Eye
www.mymindseye.com

Me and My Big Ideas
www.meandmybigideas.com

Quiet Fire Design & Lettering Art
www.quietfiredesign.com

Strathmore
www.strathmoreartist.com

Westrim Crafts
www.creativityinc.com

Embellishments

7 gypsies
www.7gypsies.com
www.sevengypsies.com

All Night Media
www.plaidonline.com

American Crafts
www.americancrafts.com

Blumenthal Lansing Company
www.buttonsplus.com

Blue Moon Beads
www.creativityinc.com

Catslife Press
www.catslifepress.com

Chatterbox
www.chatterboxinc.com

Cloud 9 Design
www.cloud9designs.biz

D. Blümchen & Company
www.blumchen.com

Die Cuts With a View
www.diecutswithaview.com

Dill Buttons
www.dill-buttons.com

EK Success
www.eksuccess.com

Frost Creek Charms
www.frostcreekcharms.com

Grandt Line Products, Inc.
www.grandtline.com

Hambly Studios
www.hamblystudios.com

Jesse James Beads–Dress It Up
www.jessejamesbeads.com

Karen Foster Design
www.karenfosterdesign.com

Lara's Crafts
www.larascrafts.com

Making Memories
www.makingmemories.com

Martha Stewart Crafts
www.marthastewartcrafts.com

Pressed Petals
www.pressedpetals.com

Provo Craft
www.provocraft.com

Ranger Industries, Inc.
www.rangerink.com

Stampington & Company
www.stampington.com

Tim Holtz
www.timholtz.com

Wrights
www.wrights.com

Collage Sheets, Images, and Rubber Stamps

Altered Pages
www.alteredpages.com

ARTchix Studio
www.artchixstudio.com

Enchanted Mercantile Vintage Graphics
www.enchantedmercantile.com

Red Letter Art, LLC
www.redletterart.com

Tallulah's Art
www.tallulahs.com

Tomorrow's Unknown
www.tomorrowsunknown.com

Victorian Scrapworks
www.victorianscrapworks.com

Stores (Online and Storefront)

A Cherry on Top
www.acherryontop.com

A.C. Moore
www.acmoore.com

Addicted to Rubber Stamps
www.addictedtorubberstamps.com

Alpha Stamps
www.alphastamps.com

Anima Designs
www.animadesigns.com

California Paper Goods
www.californiapapergoods.com

Columbus Farmer's Market
www.columbusfarmersmarket.com

Create For Less
www.createforless.com

Earth and Tree Miniatures
www.dollhouse-miniatures.com

eBay
www.ebay.com

Hancock Fabrics Online Fabric Store
www.hancockfabrics.com

Lifetime Moments
www.lifetimemoments.com

Manto Fev
www.mantofev.com

Michaels
www.michaels.com

Papier Valise
www.papiervalise.com

Pearl Art Store
www.pearlpaint.com

Scrap Lovers
store.scraplovers.com

Stamping Sensations
www.stampingsensations.com

Sunday International
www.sundayint.com

Two Peas in a Bucket
www.twopeasinabucket.com

Ribbons, Wood, and Boxes to Decorate

Maya Road
www.mayaroad.com

Morex Corp
www.morexcorp.com

Nicole Crafts
www.nicolecrafts.com

Offray Ribbon Company
www.offray.com

ABOUT THE AUTHOR

Tammy Kushnir has been an artist ever since she can remember. Her altered works have appeared in publications such as *Somerset Studio, Somerset Memories (formerly Legacy), Transparent Art, Somerset Weddings III & IV, Somerset Gallery Summers 2007 & 2008, Somerset Home,* and *Altered Arts.* Her work has appeared in *Art Journals* and *Creative Healing* by Sharon Soneff. Her drawings and mixed media work have been seen in galleries and art shows across the country. She lives in Philadelphia, Pennsylvania, with her husband and two small boys.

Email: aug2199@verizon.net
Website: www.itsmysite.com/TammyKushnir

ACKNOWLEDGMENTS

I would like to thank Mary Ann Hall for her constant belief in me. Thanks also to Winnie Prentiss, for giving me the chance to make my dream come true, and to the staff at Quayside Publishing: David, Kevin, Rosalind, and everyone else who made this possible. I would also like to thank Pat Price for all her help. I would like to say thank you to my family and friends for their constant support and encouragement. Thank you to Paul and Sue Kushnir, George and Asimina Souders, Erin and Michael Matonis, Monica and Fred Reynolds, and Gwendalynn and Madelynn McGinley, for allowing me to use their personas in my works. Last, but never least, to my husband, Mark, and my boys, Michael and Jake: You are my constant inspiration and my strength. Thank you from the bottom of my heart.